A Bluestocking Guide

World War II

by

Jane A. Williams

based on Richard J. Maybury's book
WORLD WAR II

published by
Bluestocking Press

web site: www.BluestockingPress.com
Phone 800-959-8586

Printed and bound in the United States of America.
Cover illustration by Bob O'Hara, Georgetown, CA
Cover design by Brian C. Williams, El Dorado, CA
Edited by Jane A. Williams

ISBN-10: 0-942617-59-2
ISBN-13: 978-0-942617-59-7

Published by

Bluestocking Press • Post Office Box 1014
Placerville, CA 95667-1014 • Phone: 800-959-8586
web site: www.BluestockingPress.com

Quantity Discounts Available

Books published by Bluestocking Press are available at special quantity discounts for bulk purchases to individuals, businesses, schools, libraries, and associations, to be distributed as gifts, premiums, or as fund raisers.

For terms and discount schedule contact:

Special Sales Department
Bluestocking Press
Phone: 800-959-8586
email: CustomerService@BluestockingPress.com
web site: www.BluestockingPress.com

Specify how books are to be distributed: for classrooms, or as gifts, premiums, fund raisers—or to be resold.

Contents

Chapter Title	Questions	Answers

Bluestocking Guides are designed to reinforce and enhance a student's understanding of the subject presented in the primer. The subject for this study guide is the World Wars. The primer is WORLD WAR II by Richard J. Maybury.

Given the wide range of age and ability levels of individuals who read WORLD WAR II, it is suggested that students complete the exercises in this study guide that are most age-appropriate or ability-appropriate for them.

Assignment of Exercises

While all given questions and assignments are designed to enhance the student's understanding and retention of the subject matter presented in the primer, it is by no means mandatory that each student complete every exercise in this study guide. This study guide is designed for flexibility based on a student's age, as well as a student's interest in the material presented.

It is strongly suggested that each student complete the Comprehension Exercises, but instructors can preview and then select the Application Exercises, Films to View, and Suggested Books to Read that they wish the student to complete, based on: course time available, student's interest, and/or student's age (some films/books might not be age appropriate — the student might be too young, too old, or the content too advanced for a younger student). Also, depending on the age and interest level of a student, one student might spend weeks on a research assignment, whereas another student might spend a few hours or days.

Suggested Time Frame For Study

This study guide is organized to allow the instructor flexibility in designing the ideal course of study. Therefore, there is no "right" or "wrong" time frame for covering the material; the instructor should tailor the study of the primer and study guide to the student's unique school schedule, learning style, and age. For example, younger students may only complete comprehension exercises, whereas older students may complete additional application exercises, suggested readings, and films.

An easy-to-apply rule of thumb for determining length of study is to divide the number of chapters in a primer by the number of weeks the instructor plans to study the subject/book.

Ideally, the student should read a chapter from the primer and then immediately answer the corresponding questions in the study guide. Chapter length varies, so sometimes a student may be able to read more than one chapter and complete the corresponding questions/exercises in a day. Some instructors may choose to complete the primer in a few short weeks in which case multiple chapters per day will need to be covered. Others may plan to study the primer over an entire semester, so only a few chapters per week will be assigned. The key is to move quickly enough that the student is engaged with learning and also able to absorb all concepts fully. The student's performance on end-of-chapter Questions and Assignments should be a good indication of this.

The time frame for completing application exercises (Discussion/Essay/Assignment/Research) is also subject to the instructor's discretion. Most discussions can take place immediately after reading the chapter. However, students may need a day or two to complete an essay, and some assignments will take outside research requiring additional time. It is best for the instructor to preview the application exercises (Discussion/Essay/Assignment/Research) and assign the student a "due date" based upon the student's cognitive abilities and available course schedule.

Comprehension Exercises

Comprehension Exercises test the degree to which the student understands and retains the information presented in each chapter. In this study guide Comprehension Exercises include: 1) Define, 2) True/False, and 3) Short Answer/Fill-In. Students are encouraged to answer all exercises in complete sentences. The information needed to complete these exercises can usually be found in the given chapter of the primer. Answers will be found in the answer section of this Study Guide.

Define

The student should define the given term based on Richard Maybury's definition provided in the given chapter or glossary (*not* a standard dictionary definition). This is essential. As Richard Maybury says, "Fuzzy language causes fuzzy thinking." For any discussion or explanation to be clearly understood, one must first understand the intended definition of words as used by the author. Confusion and disagreement can occur because the student does not understand the author's intended definition of a word. To reinforce this point, have a student look up the word "law" in an unabridged Webster's dictionary. The student should find a number of definitions following the word "law." Again, unless one agrees on the definition intended for the discussion or study at hand, misunderstanding or "fuzzy thinking" can result.

True/False

For True/False exercises, if the student believes the statement is correct, the student should simply write "True" as the answer. If the student believes the statement is *not* true, the student should write "False." If the student answers the question "False," the student should be sure to state why the statement is *not* true or rewrite the false statement to make it true. In the answer section of this study guide, statements that are "False" are so noted and have been rewritten to make them true.

Short Answer/Fill In

The student should answer Short Answer/Fill In questions based upon knowledge gained from studying the given chapter. Unless the student is asked to use his/her own opinion or knowledge, the answer should be based upon Richard Maybury's statements. Generally, Short Answer/Fill In Questions are selected verbatim from the given chapter.

Application Exercises

With few exceptions, Application Exercises ask the student to apply the knowledge and ideas he/she has gained from a given chapter to "real world" situations. In many cases, these assignments are designed to help the student personalize the information just learned so that the student can better retain and apply the knowledge. In this study guide application exercises include: 1) Discussion, 2) Essay, 3) Assignment, and 4) For Further Research. In the majority of instances, answers to Application Exercises will vary based upon the student's own experiences. Application Exercises are designed to encourage informal discussions among students and instructors, and/or to stimulate students to critically evaluate the scenario. However, the instructor may ask the student to write answers (in essay format, outline, etc.) if a more formal/structure approach is desired.

For Further Reading or To View

The books and films mentioned in For Further Reading and To View are designed to expand students' understanding of concepts presented in the related chapter. No written or verbal reports on the books/movies are usually required, however, students and instructors are encouraged to discuss the ideas presented. Thus, Suggestions for Further Reading/Viewing usually have no set answers and, therefore, may not appear in the "Answer" section. (The instructor may choose to assign a book/movie report of his/her own construction if he/she desires.)

How to Grade Assignments

Define, True/False, Short Answer/Fill-In

To determine the percentage of correct answers, divide the total number of correct answers by the total number of questions. If, for example, a chapter section has two Define questions, one True/False question, and seven Short Answer/Fill-In questions, and the student has answered correctly eight of these questions, the student will have answered 80% of the questions correctly.

$$8 \div 10 = .80 \text{ (or 80\%)}$$

Number of Correct Answers ÷ Number of Total Questions = Percentage of Questions Answered Correctly

In "Grade" equivalents, percentage scores generally range as follows:

90 - 100%	= A
80 - 89.9%	= B
70 - 79.9%	= C
60 - 69.9%	= D
less than 60%	= F

In general, a student earning an "A" has demonstrated excellent understanding of the subject matter; a student earning a "B" has demonstrated good understanding of the subject matter; a student earning a "C" has demonstrated sufficient understanding of the subject matter; and a student earning a "D" or "F" would benefit from reviewing the subject matter to strengthen his/her understanding of the topic at hand.

In determining whether a student has provided a "right" or "wrong" answer to a question, the instructor should compare the student's answers with the answers provided in this guide. True/False, Fill-In, and Define questions/answers are straightforward. Short Answer questions/answers are also generally straightforward; on some longer answers the student's wording may vary slightly from the answer provided in this study guide, but the student should receive full credit if the *content* of his/her answer is correct. When in doubt, it is recommended that the instructor refer back to the chapter in the primary text to reference what the author said about the issue at hand.

"Answers Will Vary"

In the answer section of this study guide you will sometimes come across an answer that reads "answers will vary" for a given question. This generally means that the student is required to answer the question using his/her own knowledge, experience, or intuition. In these instances, the instructor should refer back to the chapter in the primary text to reference what the author said about the issue at hand compared to the student's answer; a "correct" answer should be thoughtful, complete, and on-topic.

Discussion/Essay/Assignment

These assignments are provided so that students can apply the concepts they learned in the given chapter to their own experiences, current events, or historical events — to make the concepts more meaningful. In most cases, it is extremely difficult to "grade" the completed assignments as "right" or "wrong." Instead, the instructor should provide guidance for these assignments. The completeness, thoughtfulness, enthusiasm, and meaning the student brings to the assignment will serve as an indication of the student's mastery of the assignment. If the instructor then wishes to assign a grade, he/she may elect to do so. Or, these assignments may be non-graded "extra credit," serving to boost the student's overall grade for the course.

Uncle Eric's Model of How the World Works

Short Answer/Fill-In/True or False

1. What is a model as defined by Uncle Eric?

2. According to Uncle Eric, why are models important?

3. Why is it important to sort incoming data?

4. Are models rigid? Should they ever change?

5. What are the two models Uncle Eric believes are most reliable, as well as crucially important for everyone to learn? Why does he believe this?

6. _____ is the political philosophy that is no philosophy at all. It embraces the concept that those in power can do whatever appears necessary to achieve their goals.

Discussion/Essay/Assignment

7. Other than Uncle Eric's model, can you provide other examples of models?

8. What purpose does the book WORLD WAR II have relative to Uncle Eric's Model?

9. Listen to, or read, politicians' political speeches, news conferences, news releases, etc., and note if, or how often, the politicians use the phrase "we will do whatever is necessary" to execute a proposal, fix a problem, etc. Do you think it is ever okay to "do whatever is necessary" to resolve a problem? Explain your answer.

10. Look up several of the following words in a dictionary and read their definitions: fascism, liberty, economics, history, republic, and democracy. Does each word have more than one definition? Why?

11. If a word has more than one definition, why is it important that an author define his/her meaning of a word about which he/she is writing?

12. Richard Feynman, a Nobel prize winning physicist, once said it didn't matter what something was called, so long as one understood the characteristics that go into making up what that thing is. It doesn't matter if we call the bird identified as a Blue Jay, a "Blue Jay," so long as we understand that the living creature called by that name has the following characteristics: The bird's food consists primarily of nuts and small seeds as well as insects. They lay from three to six eggs that are blue, green, or yellow with spots of brown or gray. They live for about four years. Another example might be: You might have different names during your lifetime, but you are still the same person. When you are born your parents might name you William. As a child, you might be Billy, or you might

be given a nickname (i.e. Laura Ingalls Wilder from the LITTLE HOUSE™ books was called Half-pint by her Pa). As a teenager you might be Bill or Will, then, as an adult, you might use the more formal William. In all these cases, with all these names, you are still you. If you are female, you might have a maiden name and a married name. Do you agree or disagree with Richard Feynman? Does it matter what something is called, so long as one understands the characteristics of the thing? Explain and provide support for your position.

For Further Reading

13. Read CAPITALISM FOR KIDS by Karl Hess for additional information on different political philosophies, particularly the chapter called "Capitalism and Other Isms." Published by Bluestocking Press, web site: www.BluestockingPress.com; Phone: 800-959-8586.

Author's Disclosure

Short Answer/Fill-In/True or False

1. What is Juris Naturalism?

Discussion/Essay/Assignment

2. In the "Author's Disclosure," Richard Maybury says that few writers disclose the viewpoints or opinions they use to decide what information is important and what is not, or what data will be presented and what data omitted. Collect several history books from your home library, school library, or public library. Do the authors of the books you collected disclose their viewpoints or opinions to the reader? Do the authors disclose what criteria they used to determine what information or data to include in the book and what to omit? Explain why it is, or is not, important to have biases disclosed. What benefit, if any, does a reader or viewer have (in the case of movies, televised news, or documentaries) if he/she is able to determine the viewpoint of a writer?

3. Uncle Eric says all history is slanted based on the facts historians choose to report. Can you provide examples of material you have read or to which you have listened where facts have been reported but perhaps not all the facts? If no books come to mind, have you had arguments or disagreements between siblings or friends in which, when asked, each person presented his/her side of the argument—presenting only those facts that best favored his/her side of the story? How can you learn to identify the slants of writers, news commentators, friends, etc.?

4.   Read the quotes in the "Author's Disclosure" section of this book that help to describe the Juris Naturalist viewpoint. Look up the definition of "unalienable" in a current dictionary. Compare a current dictionary's definition with the definition from NOAH WEBSTER'S 1828 DICTIONARY: "Unalienable; that cannot be legally or justly alienated or transferred to another ... All men have certain natural rights which are inalienable."

5.   Samuel Adams defined the natural rights of the colonists as the right to life, liberty, and property. Why do you think "property" was changed to "happiness" in the Declaration of Independence? *(Optional exercise: You can turn this into a research exercise by researching primary source documents of America's Founders to see if you can find the answer for the change from "property" to "happiness." Provide support for your position.)*

6.   Select one of the quotes from the "Author's Disclosure" section of this book and write a short essay about what the quote means to you.

For Further Reading

7.   Read HOW TO LIE WITH STATISTICS by Darrell Huff, published by W.W. Norton, and distributed by Bluestocking Press, web site: www.BluestockingPress.com; Phone: 800-959-8586. Excellent book. A modern classic. Shows how statistics can distort truth. For ages 14 and up.

8.   Read EVALUATING BOOKS: WHAT WOULD THOMAS JEFFERSON THINK ABOUT THIS? an Uncle Eric book by Richard J. Maybury. This book provides key indicators and terms to help the reader learn how to identify the slants of authors, media commentators, and others. Published by Bluestocking Press, web site: www.BluestockingPress.com; Phone: 800-959-8586. For ages 12 and up.

9.   Visit www.worldpress.org on the Internet. Many articles posted on this site list the author and his/her philosophical viewpoint, i.e., Centrist, Libertarian, Liberal, Conservative. Have someone cover up the name and philosophical identity of each author and then read the articles. Can you identify each author's philosophical viewpoint? For help with this exercise, if a student has limited knowledge of political and economic biases, the student should first read Richard J. Maybury's books: EVALUATING BOOKS: WHAT WOULD THOMAS JEFFERSON THINK ABOUT THIS? and ARE YOU LIBERAL? CONSERVATIVE? OR CONFUSED? published by Bluestocking Press.

Note

Web sites change often but, at the time of publication, the following web site provides hundreds of World War links, so it's a good first place to begin research.
http://www.killeenroos.com/link/war.htm

Thought Exercises

Before you begin to read WORLD WAR II, answer the following questions. Your answers should be based on your current knowledge and/or opinions. (If you have no knowledge of the issue/topic, say so.) Save your responses. You will revisit these questions at a later time. After you have answered the questions, you may begin to read WORLD WAR II.

1. Based on your current knowledge and opinions, write an essay detailing what you know about World War II. For example, what caused the war, what countries were on what side, who won, what were the results of the war, etc.

2. Explain what you know about Executive Order 9066.

3. What responsibility do you believe America has to the rest of the world today? Explain your position.

Application Exercise

Before you begin to read this book, select a country that is currently engaged in armed conflict. As you read this book, apply what you learn to events that have caused the armed conflict, as well as to events that may continue to unfold. Keep a portfolio that will contain your research, opinions, ideas, and conclusions.

For example, what caused the country to become engaged in armed conflict? What alliances, if any, has that country formed? Have any abuses of political power occurred within that country? If so, by whom, and in what way? What are the economic and legal principles on which the country is based? What type of government does the country have?

Pay attention to the words and phrases that might be used in political speeches regarding the armed conflict. Watch for emotionally charged words versus those that appeal to reason. Read media stories that cover the conflict (on the Internet, international stories can be found at www.worldpress.org).

By the time you finish reading Richard Maybury's WORLD WAR II, determine what your position is regarding the merits of the armed conflict and write an essay explaining your position. Your "Country in Armed Conflict" portfolio should be completed and given to your instructor prior to taking the final exam.

Cast of Characters

1. Complete one of the following activities:

    a. Write a biographical essay based on one of the individuals listed in the Cast of Characters.

    b. Write a one-act biographical play based on the life of an individual listed in the Cast of Characters. If you're really ambitious, perform it as well.

2. No women are listed in the Cast of Characters. Why?

3. On a piece of paper, make two columns. Title the columns as follows:

          Allies—World War II   *Axis—World War II*

Place the countries that formed each group under the appropriate heading.

The CARS Checklist for Research Source Evaluation

Credibility • Accuracy • Reasonableness • Support

The CARS checklist is designed to provide criteria for evaluating the quality and reliability of a source. By applying the CARS checklist you will be better able to separate high-quality from poor quality information to any research you conduct. You will be better prepared to critically evaluate data and expert opinions, which will better equip you to excel in school, career, and life. Read more about the CARS checklist for Research Source Evaluation at one or more of the Internet sites below. (If these sites are no longer available, then conduct an Internet search for "CARS checklist" and click on a university/college link to an explanatory article.)

http://www.virtualsalt.com/evalu8it.htm
www.ru.ac.za/library/infolit/cars.html
http://www.mhhe.com/socscience/english/allwrite3/seyler/ssite/seyler/se03/cars.mhtml

Chapter 1: The Main Theater of the War

Define

1. Allies:

2. Axis:

3. USSR:

4. Eastern Front:

Short Answer/Fill-In/True or False

5. Identify the country that suffered the greatest number of casualties among the Allied Powers. How many casualties did that country have?

6. Identify the country that suffered the greatest number of casualties among the Axis Powers. How many casualties did that country have?

7. World War II was mainly a battle between which two countries?

8. What country was caught between the two countries identified in question #7?

9. Where was the Eastern Front fought and by whom?

10. How many were killed on the Eastern Front? What percentage was this of all the deaths in the war?

11. Name the other major fronts of World War II.

12. Before reading the next chapter, "Good Guys Against Bad Guys," answer the following question: In your opinion, who were the good guys and who were the bad guys of World War II? Give reasons for your answer.

Activity

13. To better envision where the Second World War was fought and each country's casualties, spread out a world map, and on each nation's capital city, pile matchsticks to represent bodies. Let each matchstick represent 100,000 dead.

Chapter 2: Good Guys Against Bad Guys

Define

1. White hats against black hats:

Short Answer/Fill-In/True or False

2. Why does Uncle Eric say the government and the country are not the same thing?

3. To what does USG refer?

Chapter 3: Not Six Million

Define

1. Jewish Holocaust:

2. Genocide:

3. Labor camp:

4. Fascism:

5. Socialism:

Short Answer/Fill-In/True or False

6. Who, besides the Jews, did the Nazis murder?

7. Who, besides the Germans, helped murder 20.9 million people in WWII?

8. How many people did Stalin murder?

9. What did Stalin's Order #270 say? What was the effect of this order on Soviet troops?

10. What intentions did Hitler have about conquering nations?

11. What intentions did Stalin have about conquering nations?

12. In What Year was Marx's COMMUNIST MANIFESTO written?

13. What other historical, as well as economic, event took place in California the same year that Marx's COMMUNIST MANIFESTO was written?

14. In 1941, did the U.S. government know much about Hitler's genocide campaign?

15. How did this compare to the U.S. government's knowledge of Stalin's murders at that same point in time?

16. At the maximum extent of his reach what percent of the world did Hitler control and in what year was this?

17. What percent of the world had the USG's ally, the Soviet Socialists, conquered?

18. What percent of the world had the USG's ally, Britain, conquered?

19. How many people were murdered by the U.S.S.R. and China, Allied nations? How many people were murdered by Germany and Japan, Axis nations?

20. Who does Uncle Eric consider to be the good guys?

21. Before the Kremlin's empire collapsed in the 1990s, how many people did the Soviet Socialists murder?

Discussion/Essay/Assignment

22. Explain why you agree or disagree with Uncle Eric that the criteria to determine who was the most evil in World War II should be the number of innocent people murdered?

23. Explain why you believe that America was, or was not, on the side of the good guys during World War II?

For Further Reading

24. To learn more about Hitler's other genocide victims, read THE OTHER VICTIMS by Ina R. Friedman, Houghton Mifflin Co., Boston, MA 1990

Chapter 4: World War II Was Nothing New

Short Answer/Fill-In/True or False

1. Why do you think Uncle Eric gives Chris the statistics on death in this letter?

2. What does Uncle Eric believe the Second World War was about?

Discussion/Essay/Assignment

3. Explain why you agree or disagree with the following statement: "Painting Hitler as something vastly worse than the hundreds of other tyrants who have been responsible for the deaths of the other 3.4 billion draws attention away from those 3.4 billion and thereby diminishes the importance of those 3.4 billion."

4. Uncle Eric makes the following observation about government propaganda: "Here is a trick often used in propaganda. When arguing for a fight against another nation, show the evil done by that nation's rulers. When arguing to fight for another nation, show the harm done to the innocent civilians; say nothing about what the rulers are doing to civilians on the other side." If you have access to the WWII propaganda films WHY WE FIGHT, watch to see if Uncle Eric's observation is accurate, relative to these films. Also, review some of the film footage and government press conferences regarding the terrorist groups following the September 11th attacks. Is Uncle Eric correct in his observations relative to the War on Terror?

Chapter 5: Millions

Short Answer/Fill-In/True or False

1. Who did President Franklin Roosevelt side with in World War II: Japan or China, and how many people did each regime murder?

2. Why did the Chinese people rebel?

3. Who took over China in 1949?

4. What does Red in Red Chinese mean?

5. How many people did the Red Chinese murder?

6. Who was geographically closer to the United States, Germany or the Soviet Union?

7. In terms of the number of people murdered and the geographical proximity, who was the greater threat to the United States, Stalin or Hitler?

Chapter 6: Britain Was A White Hat?

Define

1. Blitz:

Short Answer/Fill-In/True or False

2. By 1940, what percentage of the world had Britain conquered?

3. What is meant by the expression, "The sun never sets on the British Empire"?

4. Did the British government obey the old British Common Law outside of its own country?

5. When did most of the deaths caused by Britain occur?

6. Explain why much of the British army and navy were not available to defend Britain in World War II.

7. Whenever the United States is asked to be involved, or becomes involved, in some foreign conflict, what question should be asked?

For Further Reading

8. Read (or review) chapters 40, 41, and 42 about the Treaty of Versailles in Richard Maybury's book WORLD WAR I: THE REST OF THE STORY.

Chapter 7: British Conquests

Short Answer/Fill-In/True or False

1. What is the meaning of the phrase, "History books are written by the victors?"

2. When did Britain first invade Ireland?

3. Did Ireland ever invade England?

4. What happens if Child A becomes friends with Child B, and Child B is the enemy of Child C? What are the chances that Child A and Child C will also become friends? Are alliances in war similar to this simple comparison?

Chapter 8: P.T. Barnum Knew

Short Answer/Fill-In/True or False

1. According to Uncle Eric, what two great gifts did the British people give the world and in what did these gifts result?

2. Why does Uncle Eric recommend the movies listed below?

3. After you watch the movies, ask yourself, do you agree with Uncle Eric that the British government was brutal, arrogant, and racist?

To View

4. Per Uncle Eric's suggestion, watch the following movies and ask yourself, "What right did the British have to be in these people's homelands? Who was the invader?" (Parental discretion is advised on all movies.)

   A. BRAVEHEART starring Mel Gibson (1995) Rated R (Parental discretion is advised.)

   B. KHARTOUM starring Charlton Heston (1966) (not rated)

   C. QUIGLEY DOWN UNDER starring Tom Selleck (1990) PG-13

   D. ZULU starring Michael Caine (1964)

Chapter 9: British Area Bombing

Define

1. Area bombing:

Short Answer/Fill-In/True or False

2. According to Uncle Eric, the British were fighting for what reasons in the world wars?

Discussion/Essay/Assignment

3. What are the differences between using concentration camps and gas chambers to murder civilians versus using airplanes to bomb civilian residential housing areas?

4. After reading this chapter on area bombing answer the following question and give your reasons to support your answer. "Were the British the good guys in World War II?"

Chapter 10: Two Questions

Short Answer/Fill-In/True or False

1. What is the effect of the camera on British rule?

2. Explain the movement called Anglo-Saxonism.

Chapter 11: When Did the War Begin?

Define

1. Blitzkrieg:

Short Answer/Fill-In/True or False

2. In 1917 what event in World War I tipped the balance against the Central Powers?

3. Why did the Germans want revenge?

4. List the nine governments that have been behind most of the worst wars since the Middle Ages.

5. In the 1930s who comprised the Allies? Were they younger or older than the Axis?

6. Who comprised the Axis by the 1930s?

7. How could the younger members of the Usual Suspects expand their empires?

8. On what date did the Germans invade Poland?

9. What date does Uncle Eric say marks the real beginning of World War II, and what event took place on that date?

10. What was the significance of the Spanish Civil War and when did it begin?

11. What was the main event of World War II?

12. Uncle Eric said that the main event of World War II was not about a battle between freedom and tyranny. What was it about?

13. With whom did the U.S. government side?

For Research

14. Ask individuals when World War II began and with what event. What percentage of those queried answered December 7, 1941, the attack on Pearl Harbor?

For Further Reading

15. FRIEDRICH by Hans Peter Richter, a Puffin book, published by Penguin. Uncle Eric says, "Ask any American when World War II began and I think most will say December 7, 1941, when the Japanese attacked Pearl Harbor. More knowledgeable ones might say September 1, 1939, when the Germans invaded Poland. Actually, the shooting started in 1931, and then increased gradually until the war was fully developed at the end of 1941." FRIEDRICH is an excellent book to help you understand how events escalated in Germany in the early 1930s.

Chapter 12: Appeasement and Comparative Brutality

Short Answer/Fill-In/True or False

1. What was the idea behind "appeasement" by the British and French governments when Germany took back the Rhineland?

2. What was the main reason that Britain and France were vulnerable to Germany?

3. In 2002, in how many countries did the U.S. government have troops stationed?

Chapter 13: Carving Up Central Europe

Define

1. Mobilize:

Short Answer/Fill-In/True or False

2. When did Hitler formally declare an end to the Treaty of Versailles?

3. When did Germany annex Austria?

4. When did Germany invade the Sudentenland in Czechoslovakia?

5. Besides Germany, what other countries grabbed pieces of Czechoslovakia in 1938?

6. What was the Soviet-German Nonaggression Pact and when was it signed?

7. What does the Hollywood version of the attack on Poland tell us?

8. Why is the Hollywood version about the attack on Poland wrong?

9. Who conquered more territory between 1919 and 1940, Berlin or Moscow?

10. The British and French declared war on Germany two days after Germany invaded Poland. Did the British or French do anything when the Soviets invaded Poland?

11. The declaration of war by Britain and France meant what to their colonies around the world?

12. When did Italy come into the war and who did Italy side with?

13. What is the Tripartite Pact?

14. What deadly idea that leads to war is represented by the Tripartite Pact?

Chapter 14: The French versus the French

Short Answer/Fill-In/True or False

1. What is the main point of Uncle Eric's letter about "The French versus the French?"

2. What is the lesson to be learned about the North African Front in 1942?

3. What was the European political philosophy that was popular for thousands of years and still popular in Europe when World War II broke out?

4. According to Uncle Eric, what two political philosophies were battling for supremacy over each other in World War II, and which won?

Chapter 15: Significance of the Higgins Boat

Short Answer/Fill-In/True or False

1. What is the significance of the Higgins boat?

2. When did the Battle of Britain end?

3. When did the Japanese attack Pearl Harbor?

4. After the Battle of Britain, what country did Hitler invade, and when?

Chapter 16: Only Genghis Khan Did It

1. Briefly, why should someone never invade Russia?

2. Who was the last person to successfully mount a winter invasion of Russia and how long did it take?

3. What is the Russian defensive strategy? Why?

4. When did the first snow fall after the German invasion of Russia?

5. How many vehicles did the Germans take into Russia in June 1941, and how many were working in November 1941?

6. According to Uncle Eric, why is September 12, 1941, the most important date of World War II?

7. When did the U.S. government enter the war?

Chapter 17: The Solution

Short Answer/Fill-In/True or False

1. Why does Uncle Eric see the attack on Russia by Hitler as the solution to the war?

2. Uncle Eric says, "Knowing the events of World War II is important. Knowing the sequence is more important." Why is this important?

Chapter 18: Events Leading to Pearl Harbor

1. Who was the chief naval power in the Orient by the 1930s?

2. What was Tokyo's plan and why?

3. Explain the Panay incident.

4. The Panay incident illustrates which of the deadly ideas that lead to war?

5. Why was the Panay incident significant?

6. Had Franklin Roosevelt violated the Neutrality Act by sending U.S. armed forces to China to protect people who had taken the risk of entering a war zone?

Chapter 19: Hiding Facts about the Brawl

Short Answer/Fill-In/True or False

1. Why does Uncle Eric say it is unlikely that anyone would attack the United States or even provoke the United States to a fight unless they believed they had no alternative?

2. What happened in 1966 to disclose information that prior to that date had been suppressed?

Discussion/Essay/Assignment

3. Before reading chapter 20 "The Great World War II Myth", answer the following questions based on your current knowledge: 1) Why did Americans fight in the Second World War? 2) What issues were Americans fighting for? 3) What is the responsibility of America to the rest of the world today?

Chapter 20: The Great World War II Myth

Discussion/Essay/Assignment

1. Now that you have finished reading "The Great World War II Myth" in what way, if any, would you change your answers to these questions: 1) Why did Americans fight in the Second World War? 2) What issues were Americans fighting for? 3) What is the responsibility of America to the rest of the world today?

2. Read Franklin Roosevelt's Pearl Harbor Speech. How do you think you would have reacted to that speech if you were hearing it live? Note: This speech, and its drafts (both printed and audio versions) are posted on the Internet at:
   http://www.archives.gov/digital_classroom/lessons/day_of_infamy/day_of_infamy.html

For Research

3. Compare and contrast Roosevelt's Day of Infamy speech to President Bush's 9-11 speech, posted on the Internet at http://www.whitehouse.gov/news/releases/2001/09/20010920-8.html

Chapter 21: A Secret Agreement

Short Answer/Fill-In/True or False

1. What was the Atlantic Charter?

2. What hidden agreement did Roosevelt make with Churchill that violated the U.S. Constitution?

3. What promise did Franklin Roosevelt make to the American people during his election campaign of 1940?

4. What did Churchill write to Roosevelt in 1939 that reveals Churchill's desire for power?

5. How much of the world did Britain control in 1939?

Chapter 22: Why did the Japanese Attack?

Define

1. Logistics:

Short Answer/Fill-In/True or False

2. Why are logistics important in a war?

3. In 1941 who was the chief supplier of oil, iron, and other necessary resources to Japan?

4. Before reading the next chapter, "Pearl Harbor, FDR's Deceit," explain why you think the Japanese would attack the United States, the most powerful industrial nation in the world, the nation they were most dependent on for resources and products, and the nation that could outfight the Japanese? Save your answer. You will revisit it.

Discussion/Essay/Assignment

5. The commander of the Pearl Harbor attack force, Admiral Yamamoto, said, "I fear we have awakened a sleeping giant and filled him with a terrible resolve." Compare this statement by Yamamoto to the actions taken by the U.S. government following the September 11th attacks.

6. Uncle Eric says, "The American way of fighting a war was (still is) to hit the enemy with a deluge of ships, planes, tanks, and artillery—to overwhelm them with machinery." Is Uncle Eric's observation relevant to America's War on Terror?

Chapter 23: Pearl Harbor, FDR's Deceit

Define

1. Freeze:

2. Expeditionary force:

Short Answer/Fill-In/True or False

3. In 1940, what percent of Americans opposed the U.S. getting involved in the war?

4. Who was placed in charge of all intelligence information about Japan that was routed to President Roosevelt?

5. Did McCollum want the U.S. to get into the war? What were his reasons?

6. What was McCollum's eight-point plan intended to do?

7. Uncle Eric lists the steps in McCollum's Eight-Point Plan, the chronological order of events, and the number of the step to which a chronological event corresponds. Were any of the steps in the Eight-Point Plan not executed by some event?

8. List the steps in McCollum's Eight-Point Plan and the chronological event/s that corresponds to each step, proving the plan was executed. An example of how to do this follows:

McCollum's Eight-Point Plan

Step 1: Get permission from the British to put U.S. ships in Britain's Pacific bases, especially Singapore (near the oil fields of the Dutch East Indies, which are now called Indonesia).
> 4 Oct 1940. Churchill gives permission to put U.S. warships in Singapore, which is near the oil fields of the Dutch East Indies (Indonesia).

9. According to Uncle Eric, on what date did the war turn in favor of the Allies? Why the turn of events? Why was this significant?

10. Now that you've read this chapter, "Pearl Harbor, FDR's Deceit," review your answer to the question: Why do you think the Japanese would attack the United States, the most powerful industrial nation in the world, the nation they were most dependent on for resources and products, and the nation that could outfight the Japanese? Would you make any changes to your answer. If so, explain why.

Chapter 24: The Flying Tigers and B-17 Bombers

Short Answer/Fill-In/True or False

1. What was the official name of the Flying Tigers?

2. What was the official story about who hired the Flying Tigers and when?

3. What was the truth about whom the Flying Tigers worked for?

4. What was significant about who the Flying Tigers really worked for?

5. Where was the entire factory production of the B-17 Flying Fortress located?

To View

6. THE FLYING TIGERS (1942) starring John Wayne. Story of Flying Tigers stationed in China.

7. THIRTEEN DAYS (2000) starring Kevin Costner. Story of the 1962 Cuban missile crisis. Rated PG-13. As you watch, consider the reactions of the United States government to the arms buildup in Cuba and compare that to the reaction of the Japanese to the arms buildup in the Philippines during World War II.

Chapter 25: "Caught With Their Pants Down"

Short Answer/Fill-In/True or False

1. Who warned Roosevelt about a possible attack on Pearl Harbor?

2. What was the root cause for concern over a possible attack on Pearl Harbor?

3. Did Roosevelt give Kimmel the additional firepower Kimmel wanted?

4. From the beginning of the attack, how long did it take Kimmel to get all guns firing?

5. If Kimmel got all his guns firing so quickly, how were the Japanese able to cause so much damage?

Discussion/Essay/Assignment

6. Kimmel received many "war warnings" for seventeen months prior to the attack on Pearl Harbor. There was nothing knew in the November 27th, 1941 message to indicate it had greater importance than any other. Since the September 11th attacks the American public have received several varying levels of terrorist alert warnings. Have individuals become complacent about these terrorist warnings? How do you think anyone will be able to recognize a "real" warning? Does this comparison help you to better understand Kimmel's position?

Chapter 26: Planes Parked Too Close Together

Short Answer/Fill-In/True or False

1. How does a commander guard against air attack?

2. How does a commander guard against sabotage and espionage?

3. Why did Kimmel and Short park their planes close together and in the open?

4. What percent of the population of Hawaii was of Japanese descent?

Discussion/Essay/Assignment

5. If you were Kimmel, what strategy would you have used to protect your ships and planes with the information made available to you at that time?

Chapter 27: The Prokofiev Seamount

Short Answer/Fill-In/True or False

1. What is significant about the Prokofiev Seamount in November 1941?

2. Why were only older ships in Pearl Harbor at the time of the Japanese attack?

3. How many anti-aircraft guns did the Arizona have compared to the battleship Washington, the latter ship being one that was sent away from Pearl Harbor?

4. From where did the Japanese launch their planes?

Chapter 28: The Necessary Sacrifice?

Short Answer/Fill-In/True or False

1. What is the "Necessary Sacrifice" explanation about the attack on Pearl Harbor?

2. What is the flaw in the "Necessary Sacrifice" explanation?

3. What is Executive Order No. 9066? On what date was it signed?

4. What percentage of Japanese placed in U.S. concentration camps were U.S. citizens?

5. Was placing these Japanese in concentration camps constitutional?

6. Was any government official ever prosecuted for internment of the Japanese?

Discussion/Essay/Assignment

7. Answer the following questions and provide reasons for your opinions: Should I always have faith in my government? If not, when should I question my government? When should I disobey my government? (Do you think America's Founders went through this same self-examination process when trying to determine if they had the right to rebel against England? What about: Abolitionists who helped slaves escape on the Underground Railroad? Citizens of Nazi occupied European countries that helped Jewish people hide or escape?)

8. Although not usually heard about, other nationalities besides Japanese were targeted by the U.S. government and placed in camps. Select one of these alternative groups and write a short essay about what you can find out about their internment experiences. (For example, Italian-Americans and German-Americans were also placed in internment camps.) Here are two web sites to get you started:
   http://www.serve.com/shea/germusa/itintern.htm
   http://www.indianamilitary.org/ATTERBURYPOW/ItalianInfo/ItalianCorrespondence.htm

For Further Reading

9. ROY UYEDA'S STORY, (see next page) a personal account of Roy Uyeda that details the violations of U.S. Constitution rights by the U.S. government during World War II against Japanese-American soldiers.

10. JOURNEY TO TOPAZ by Yoshiko Uchida. Yuki, 11 years old, is shipped to the desert concentration camp called Topaz. Based on the author's personal experience. Ages 10 and up. Published by Creative Arts Book Company.

11. FAREWELL TO MANZANAR by Jeanne Wakatsuki Houston & James D. Houston. True story of a Japanese-American family's attempt to survive the indignities of forced detention at Manzanar. Ages 12 and up. Published by Dell Laurel-Leaf, New York.

Roy Uyeda
Japanese-American in WWII

(printed with permission of Roy Uyeda)

I was born on April 14, 1920. I attended Loomis Grammar School (California) where it seemed like I was picked on a lot. The bullies would take my lunch and sort through it and toss it in the garbage. I was only 4' 9" when I graduated from Loomis and then I went to Placer High, where discrimination seemed to follow me. I transferred to Roseville High for my senior year and there was no discrimination at all.

On November 4, 1941, I was drafted and sent to Monterey. I enlisted in the Air Corps Cadet training program on November 11, 1941 where I was promised training as a pilot. I had fantasized on being a pilot. I was sent to Jefferson Barracks where the squadron I was in awaited orders for cadet training—and my usual good luck followed —December 7,1941.

I was immediately put in the Brig. There were no charges against me. This was a very traumatic period. I didn't know if I was going to face a firing squad. Twice a day, I was dogtrotted to chow with a bayonet at my butt. After chow, I was frisked for knives or forks before having the cell door clanged shut. Humiliation! Wearing Uncle Sam's uniform didn't mean a thing.

On February 2, 1942, I was sent with an armed guard, on secret orders, to Brooks Field, Texas. There a civilian named Alice S. took my service records. Several months later she came to me to apologize. She said that she noted on my record that I was Japanese. Having never seen anyone like that before, she envisioned the GIs with knives in their backs with me around. Thanks to Walter Winchell and his cohort newscasters for their propaganda stirring things up.

My dad and father-in-law were interned in 1942 at Bismarck, North Dakota. They rejoined the family at Tule Lake in 1943. Then they all were transferred to Jerome, Arkansas, and then to Heart Mountain, Wyoming. The family of my wife, Grace Otani (her mother was Savaye Otani), was sent to Amache, Colorado.

In October of 1943, I was transferred to the 442 Regimental Combat Team. I told the commanding officer that I had enlisted in the Air Corp. This fell on deaf ears.

The 442 R.C.T. was formed to show that the Japanese were loyal to the U.S. government. The government went to the Japanese concentration camps and asked for volunteers to form this unit. Imagine this. You have been uprooted from your homes, allowed to take two bundles of possessions, and you don't know where you are going or for how long. Everything else you own is stored. (Looters had a field day.) Your assets sold for a penny on the dollar. You are put behind barbed wire with no respect for your constitutional rights. No charges were ever pressed. You are issued a 4-C draft card, which means you are an enemy alien. Now they ask you to be loyal and volunteer for military service. Talk about patriotism. I take my hat off to them. How would you react to this? Six thousand men volunteered for military intelligence service. They were sent to the South Pacific to interrogate prisoners. Some went into caves to ask the enemy to surrender. Pretty gutsy.

Fifteen hundred more men volunteered for the 442 Regimental Combat Team from the concentration camps and 2,100 volunteers came from Hawaii.

The 442 R.C.T. faced discrimination. Its first battalion was halted before entering Rome, Italy. We sat on the roadside while the Caucasian troops moved in and got credit for liberating Rome.

A second humiliating event occurred in France. The 36th Division from Texas could not penetrate into the Vosges Mountains in Eastern France. (This was the last stronghold before entering Germany.) The 442nd was called in to take Bruyeres, which was the gateway to Vosges. There was a lot of hand-to-hand combat, room by room, building by building. The 442nd suffered heavy casualties, but we cleared the city of Germans. Here's what hurt. General Dalquist, the commander of the 36th division, which we literally saved, told our commander that he could not acknowledge our presence in this action due to censorship—his own censorship. News came out in the U.S. that the 36th Division had gained a foothold in the Vosges Mountains. We weren't mentioned. These incidents are only a couple of the discriminations that the 442nd faced. We were a dispensable unit. When the going was impossible, call in the 442nd.

We suffered over 312% casualties (some soldiers were injured several times) and we were the highest decorated Regiments in the history of U.S. Army records. Because we were put in to the toughest situations, the Army had no choice but to recognize what the 442nd had done.

For the record, my friend Wilson Makabe left his legs in Italy. He and two brothers in the service had their home, located across Granite Drive from Sierra College (California), torched. Omachi's home on High Cliff Road was also burned. Twenty-nine families never returned to Loomis because they lost everything. Many, like my parents, recovered their property but lost all other assets to looters.

Yes, Loomis has its share of blemished history. Shortly after the war ended I'm reminded of the late Homer Takahashi's statement: "We came home to a hero's welcome—'No Japs Allowed' signs plastered all over." Ironic isn't it? We put our lives on the line to protect the lives of these people who put up all of the hate signs.

President Reagan issued an apology for the government in denying us our constitutional rights with no charges. This apology restored my faith that this is the greatest country in the world, and with a change in the generation, Loomis is once again a nice place to call home.

My wound has healed but the scar remains as a reminder that this should never ever happen again. I feel sorry and also obligated to the few Caucasian friends who stood by us during this time. Shamefully, they were ostracized as "Jap" lovers. This, my friends, is part of Loomis' history.

• • •

Roy Uyeda (1920-2004) often spoke to school children and adults about his experiences in World War II. He was a docent for the Japanese American Citizens Leagues' Time of Remembrance project. Roy Uyeda believed it was essential that the lessons learned from the mass incarceration of Japanese Americans, without due process, never be forgotten—so that such injustices would never happen again.

Chapter 29: You've Seen the Photos

Short Answer/Fill-In/True or False

1. How long after the Japanese attack on Pearl Harbor began did the battleship Arizona explode?

Discussion/Essay/Assignment

2. Do you think it was a coincidence that a movie camera was set up to capture the explosion on film?

Chapter 30: The Myth of German Might

Define

1. Napalm:

Short Answer/Fill-In/True or False

2. What is the Hollywood version of history about Hitler and Germany?

3. When studying the economics of war, what exactly is being studied?

4. Why is the story of the Panzer Lehr Division important?

5. Who changed sides from the Axis to the Allies in 1943?

Chapter 31: Focus on the Eastern Front

Define

1. Division:

Short Answer/Fill-In/True or False

2. Who was fighting whom in the Pacific Theater?

3. Who was fighting whom in the European Theater?

4. What was the main battlefield of the war?

5. Where was the worst battle in history fought and how many died?

6. What was the biggest battle on the Western Front and how many died?

7. How did casualties from these two worst battles on these two fronts compare?

8. What was the single largest military operation in all of human history?

Chapter 32: Of Photographs and Weather

For Discussion and Research

1. Uncle Eric tells Chris that one reason for the lack of film footage about the Eastern Front might be because it was harder to film in snowstorms and across vast expanses of ground. Also, Americans have less interest in films about Germans fighting Russians. If you are interested in researching this, check some film guides and see how many films have been made about the Western Front versus the Eastern Front.

To View

2. ENEMY AT THE GATES (2001) starring Jude Law and Ed Harris. A Russian sharpshooter is marketed as a hero to bolster the country's morale during the days surrounding the Battle of Stalingrad. Also a good example of guerrilla warfare and how many troops are needed to restrain one marksman. Rated R. Parental discretion advised.

Chapter 33: German Production of Weapons

Define

1. Strategic:

Short Answer/Fill-In/True or False

2. Why did Germany excel at the beginning of the war?

3. Add the Allied total populations together and compare the totals to Germany's total? What conclusion/s can you draw?

4. Compare the populations of Germany, the Soviet Union, and Britain.

5. How many additional people comprised the British colonies?

6. When did Hitler attack Stalin?

7. Strategically, could Hitler beat both Russia and Britain?

8. What is significant about Congresswoman Jeannette Rankin?

9. What is the significant point being made in this letter?

For Research

10. Research and write an essay on Jeannette Rankin.

Chapter 34: Germany's Unknown Second Army

Short Answer/Fill-In/True or False

1. What two armies did Germany have?

2. How many tanks did Hitler have with which to invade Russia and how many did Stalin have?

3. Why did the Russians receive such a beating in the beginning of the invasion of Russia?

4. Uncle Eric says that once you understand the economics of the World War II you would see what others do not. What does he mean?

Chapter 35: Tank Treads, Trucks, and Submarines

Short Answer/Fill-In/True or False

1. Why are the treads of German tanks important?

2. What production mistake did Hitler make in World War II?

3. In November 1941, before the U.S. entered the war, what percent of Hitler's tank division was still running?

4. What was the weakness of Panzer I and Panzer II tanks?

5. What was the weakness of the first German Tiger tank?

6. What is Uncle Eric's main point about German weaponry?

Chapter 36: Germany's Wonder Weapons

Define

1. Prototype:

Short Answer/Fill-In/True or False

2. The Hollywood version of history says that Germany's scientists and engineers were developing advanced technologies that would obliterate the Allies if the USG did not enter the war. What's the other side of story?

3. What role did Hitler play in the development of weaponry?

Chapter 37: Oil and Rifles

Short Answer/Fill-In/True or False

1. Why does Uncle Eric place so much emphasis on acquisition of oil in World War II?

2. What percentage of oil did the Allies control and what percent did the Axis control in World War II?

3. What can be said about the Japanese and Italian weaponry?

4. Was Germany primarily a land or sea power?

Chapter 38: Americans Were Less Intelligent?

Short Answer/Fill-In/True or False

1. What can be said about the P-51 Mustang and the production capabilities of America during World War II?

2. What can be said about the B-24 and the production capabilities of building it?

3. How did Germany's production capability of bombers compare to America's?

4. How many heavy bombers did the Japanese have?

5. By 1944 what material was the German Heinkel 162 jet fighter mostly made of and why?

6. In what ratio was America outproducing Japan, Germany, and Italy combined by the end of 1942?

7. What was the main cargo ship of WWII?

8. How many aircraft carriers were built during World War II in America? How many did Germany build?

Chapter 39: The Brookings Revelation

Short Answer/Fill-In/True or False

1. What did the June 1941 Brookings Institution report have to say about Germany's ability to produce weapons and supplies?

2. What is significant about the date of the report?

3. What was a key reason the Third Reich lost the war?

Chapter 40: Russia Invaded by Keystone Kops

Short Answer/Fill-In/True or False

1. What are logistics and why are logistics important to the outcome of a war?

2. What did the Russians do to foil an attempt by a foreign country to invade Russia by rail?

3. How did the German invasion of Russia differ from a normal invasion of a country?

4. The Eastern Front was what percent of the war and how important was Hitler's success or failure in Russia?

Chapter 41: Omaha Beach, Bravery versus Heroism

Define

1. Berlin Wall:

Short Answer/Fill-In/True or False

2. When was D-Day?

3. What do most people think was the reason for the invasion of Normandy?

4. What was the real purpose behind the invasion of Normandy?

5. What was the result for the world because of the invasion of Normandy?

For Research and Further Reading

6. In this chapter, Uncle Eric discusses how the enemy is dehumanized, seen as a vicious animal who deserves to be killed, which make it easier for a soldier to fight the enemy and the people on the home front to support the war.   Insulting names, caricatures, and cartoons are some of the vehicles used to accomplish this. For examples, secure a copy of DR. SEUSS GOES TO WAR: THE WORLD WAR II EDITORIAL CARTOONS OF THEODOR SEUSS GEISEL, text and compilation by Richard H. Minear, published by The New Press, NY, copyright 1999.
Some of Geisel's editorial cartoons can be found on the Internet at:
http://orpheus.ucsd.edu/speccoll/dspolitic/

7. On the Internet visit: www.WorldPress.org and click on the link to "World in Cartoons" for contemporary international political cartoons. You will very likely see some that are not favorable to U.S. foreign policy. Discuss some of these cartoons with your teacher. How does it make you feel when you see the U.S. government made the brunt of political cartoons by foreign presses?

8. If you can get access to this DVD, watch ON THE FRONT LINES by Walt Disney Treasures, (ISBN 0-7888-5070-9). This is a very interesting example of what the folks at home were watching while World War II raged.   In an effort to win their hearts and minds, the Walt Disney Studios turned out these cartoons for the government during World War II. Watch how frequently war themes are interwoven into what otherwise should be informative educational cartoons (i.e., a cartoon on becoming vaccinated). Watch *Education for Death* about compulsory education under the Nazis. Also watch the Academy Award winning *Der Fuerher's Face*.

9. Poster art was used to persuade the public to support the war. View them on the Internet at:
www.library.northwestern.edu/govpub/collections/wwii-posters/
www.archives.gov/exhibit_hall/powers_of_persuasion/powers_of_persuasion_intro.html
www.trumanlibrary.org/museum/posters/

Chapter 42: The German Underground

Short Answer/Fill-In/True or False

1. What percent of the vote did Hitler receive in the 1932 election?

2. What is the Hollywood version of the liberation of France as opposed to the side of the story told by Uncle Eric?

3. Did Germans try to assassinate Hitler?

4. Did the German resistance seek aid from the Allies to fight against Hitler and, if so, what was the result?

5. Why did the Treaty of Versailles cause some Germans to not join or not assist the German resistance?

6. What happened to General Erwin Rommel?

For Further Reading

7. HITLER'S GERMAN ENEMIES by Louis L. Snyder, published by Hippocrene Books, NY, 1990.

Chapter 43: Unconditional Surrender

Short Answer/Fill-In/True or False

1. What did the Moscow Declaration say?

2. When was the Battle of Stalingrad and what was significant about it?

3. When did Franklin Roosevelt call for Unconditional Surrender?

4. Are surrenders normally conditional or unconditional, and what does unconditional mean?

5. What effect might an Unconditional Surrender have on an enemy's willingness to surrender?

6. What effect did the Unconditional Surrender have on extending the war?

7. When Germany did surrender unconditionally, what happened to the three million German prisoners of war that were sent to Russia?

8. What was the one other historic case of Unconditional Surrender that Churchill's advisor, Lord Maurice Hankey, found? What happened to the loser?

9. Besides the fear of death, what was the other main reason that the anti-Nazis were negotiating for a conditional surrender?

For Research

10. Research the war between the Romans and the Carthaginians, specifically the surrender terms and results.

Chapter 44: Why Did Roosevelt Do It?

Short Answer/Fill-In/True or False

1. Why did Roosevelt ignore several opportunities to end the war early, according to Uncle Eric?

2. Did Harry Truman maintain the demand for Unconditional Surrender?

Chapter 45: Rarely Questioned

Short Answer/Fill-In/True or False

1. List the ten Deadly Ideas that lead to war.

2. What is significant about these ten Deadly Ideas?

Chapter 46: Why Was Nagasaki Bombed?

Short Answer/Fill-In/True or False

1. The Hollywood and U.S. government versions of history contain what two assumptions about the end of WWII?

2. What is the non-statist explanation?

3. When did the atomic bomb drop on Nagasaki and when did Foreign Minister Togo and Emperor Hirohito decide to ask the Japanese War Council to announce Japan's surrender?

Chapter 47: 105 Aircraft Carriers

Short Answer/Fill-In/True or False

1. What is the statist side of the story about the need to bomb Japan with atomic bombs?

2. Did the U.S. government use area bombing? Explain.

Chapter 48: Surrender Near

For Discussion

1. Admiral Leahy believed that it was unnecessary to drop the atomic bomb on Japan. He believed Japan was already defeated with conventional weapons and a sea blockade. Leahy said, "In being the first to use it (the atomic bomb), we had adopted an ethical standard common to the barbarians of the Dark Age." Explain why you agree or disagree with Leahy's statement and support your answer.

Chapter 49: Fierce Fighters

Define

1. Cold War:

Short Answer/Fill-In/True or False

2. Why didn't the Japanese surrender? What caused them to fight so fiercely, even when they knew they were defeated?

3. What is the reason cited by journalist Peter Wyden in his book DAY ONE, for the atomic bombing of Japan?

4. When did Truman halt Lend Lease aid to the USSR? Why is this date significant?

5. Why did the U.S. government drop the bomb on Nagasaki so quickly?

Chapter 50: The Russians React

Short Answer/Fill-In/True or False

1. What was the result of World War I on the Russian people?

2. What political party came into power as the result of the 1917 Russian Revolution?

3.   Who were the "wreckers" and what happened to them?

Chapter 51: The Soviet Uprising

Short Answer/Fill-In/True or False

1. Why didn't the Soviet people rebel against their own government during World War II like they had during World War I?

2. What was Operation Keelhaul?

3. When did Soviet troops invade Afghanistan?

4. When did the Soviet Empire begin to collapse?

Chapter 52: Arm Any Gangster

Short Answer/Fill-In/True or False

1. Who emerged as the most powerful person in the Old World following World War II?

2. How much land did Stalin directly control following World War II?

3. What was the Truman Doctrine?

4. At the time this book was written, how many governments throughout the world received U.S. assistance?

5. Of the more than 200 countries in the world, how many have governments limited enough to make an American want to live in that country?

6. In an attempt to prevent the rise of another Hitler, what action did the U.S. government take following World War II?

7. By the year 2000 how many countries did the U.S. sphere of influence include?

8. What is the root cause of terrorist attacks against the U.S.?

For Research

9. The U.S. government provided money, military training, or other assistance to the following list of people. Select one for research and write a short report. You might begin your research on the Internet at: http://users.erols.com/mwhite28/tyrants.htm

>   Osama bin Laden in Afghanistan
>   Fidel Castro in Cuba
>   Saddam Hussein in Iraq
>   President Diem of Vietnam
>   The Shah of Iran
>   General Zia ul-Haq in Pakistan
>   Marcos in the Philippines
>   Manuel Noriega in Panama
>   Mobutu in the Congo
>   Chiang Kai-shek in Taiwan
>   General Park Chung-hee in Korea
>   Suharto and Habibie in Indonesia

Chapter 53: September 11th

Discussion/Essay/Assignment

1. Uncle Eric says that the USG's support for tyrants around the world left millions of victims with grudges that resulted in the World Trade Center attacks. Do you agree or disagree and why?

2. President Bill Clinton sent aid to the Kremlin when Russian troops were fighting Muslim Chechens. What effect do you think this had on how Muslims perceived the U.S. government?

3. After the September 11th attacks, Americans began to hear, perhaps for the first time, in news interviews with terrorist experts that many foreigners hated America. Do you recall when the first time was that you heard that people in foreign countries hated America?

For Research

4. With money, weapons, military training, or some other kind of aid, the U.S. government has helped the governments of Russia, Egypt, Macedonia, Romania, Kazakhstan, Uzbekistan, Saudi Arabia, Chad, Nigeria, and Columbia. Select one of these countries and write a report about its political, legal, and economic history. You might start by visiting on the Internet: http://www.amnestyusa.org/arms_trade/controlarms_summary.html
    Here you will learn that "the five permanent members of the UN Security Council - France, Russia, China, the UK, and the USA - together account for 88 per cent of the world's conventional arms exports; and these exports contribute regularly to gross abuses of human rights."

For Further Reading

5. THE THOUSAND YEAR WAR IN THE MIDEAST: HOW IT AFFECTS YOU TODAY, by Richard J. Maybury, published by Bluestocking Press, web site: www.BluestockingPress.com, phone: 800-959-8586.

Chapter 54: Blowback

Define

1. Blowback:

For Research and Discussion

2. Research other terrorist attacks throughout the world. How does the September 11th attacks compare to what has happened in other places?

Chapter 55: MAD

Define

1. MAD:

Short Answer/Fill-In/True or False

2. When did the USSR detonate the H-bomb and how powerful was it compared to the A-bomb?

To View

3. THIRTEEN DAYS (2000) starring Kevin Costner. Story of the 1962 Cuban missile crisis. Rated PG-13. Demonstrates the fear the U.S. had of Russia.

Chapter 56: Police Officers of the World

Define

1. No-fly zone:

Short Answer/Fill-In/True or False

2. Read the quote from George Washington's Farewell Address that appears on page one of Richard Maybury's WORLD WAR II. What was Washington's position regarding foreign policy?

3. What are the two laws that make peace, liberty, and prosperity possible?

Discussion/Essay/Assignment

4. Write a brief essay explaining the difference between isolationism and neutrality.

5. Watch for the words "isolationism" and "isolationist" in media broadcasts and history books. Is the distinction ever made between those terms and "neutrality?" Is the term isolationist used in a positive or negative way?

6. Post these two laws in a prominent place in your home: 1) Do all you have agreed to do, and 2) do not encroach on other persons or their property. Whenever a disagreement or problem arises, review the two laws and determine which, if any, has been violated. Also, note how often disagreements arise because a clear understanding of what one was agreeing to do was never fully understood.

Chapter 57: Summary

Discussion/Essay/Assignment

1. Summarize the story that is generally taught to Americans about how the U.S. got into World War II and the consequences of that war.

2. What actions has the U.S. government taken since World War II that has resulted in terrorist attacks against the U.S. today?

3. Give your opinion about Uncle Eric's four-point plan. Do you think it would have worked? Why or why not? Where might it be improved upon?

Chapter 58: The Needless Deaths of 35 Million

Discussion/Essay/Assignment

1. Make a list of questions you would ask before you would be willing to march off to war.

2. Uncle Eric gives Chris the reasons under which he would be willing to risk his life in war. Where do you agree or differ with Uncle Eric?

Chapter 59: The Normal Condition of Humans

Define

1. Fungible:

Short Answer/Fill-In/True or False

2. What is the effect of foreign aid sent for humanitarian purposes, i.e. food, blankets, clothing?

Chapter 60: The Cause of War

Short Answer/Fill-In/True or False

1. According to Uncle Eric, what were the world wars about?

Chapter 61: Minor League to Emperor of the World

Short Answer/Fill-In/True or False

1. Why does Uncle Eric think the rest of the story about the World Wars is not widely known?

2. What is Uncle Eric's advice regarding American foreign policy?

Thought Exercises Revisited

Before you began to read WORLD WAR II you were asked to provide answers to the following:

1. Based on your current knowledge and opinions, write an essay detailing what you know about World War II. For example, what caused the war, what countries were on what side, who won, what were the results of the war, etc.

2. Explain what you know about Executive Order 9066.

3. What responsibility do you believe America has to the rest of the world today? Explain your position.

Now that you have finished reading Richard J. Maybury's book WORLD WAR II, review your answers to the Thought Exercises. Would you make any changes to your answers? Explain what changes you would make and why. If you would make no changes, explain why you are satisfied with your answers as previously written. If you did not originally provide an answer for lack of knowledge, answer the exercises now.

Application Exercise

Complete and turn in your "Country in Armed Conflict"
portfolio to your instructor at this time.

Final Exam Questions

1. Define: Allies

2. Define: Axis

3. Identify the country that suffered the greatest number of casualties among the Allied Powers. About how many casualties did that country have?

4. Identify the country that suffered the greatest number of casualties among the Axis Powers. About how many casualties did that country have?

5. World War II was mainly a battle between which two countries?

6. Where was the Eastern Front fought and by whom?

7. How many were killed on the Eastern Front? What percentage was this of all the deaths in the war?

8. Name the other major fronts of World War II.

9. Define: Fascism

10. Define: Socialism

11. Who, besides the Jews, did the Nazis murder?

12. According to Uncle Eric, who murdered more people, Stalin or Hitler?

13. What did Stalin's Order #270 say? What was the effect of this order on Soviet troops?

14. What intentions did Hitler have about conquering nations?

15. What intentions did Stalin have about conquering nations?

16. At the maximum extent of his reach, what percent of the world did Hitler control and in what year was this?

17. What percent of the world had the USG's ally, the Soviet Socialists, conquered?

18. What percent of the world had the USG's ally, Britain, conquered?

19. Who did President Franklin Roosevelt side with in World War II: Japan or China, and how many people did each regime murder?

20. Who took over China in 1949 and how many people did they murder?

21. In terms of the number of people murdered and the geographical proximity, who was the greater threat to the United States, Stalin or Hitler?

22. What is meant by the expression, "The sun never sets on the British Empire"?

23. Explain why much of the British army and navy were not available to defend Britain in World War II?

24. What is the meaning of the phrase, "History books are written by the victors?"

25. According to Uncle Eric, what two great gifts did the British people give the world and in what did these gifts result?

26. Explain the movement called Anglo-Saxonism.

27. Define: Blitzkrieg

28. In 1917 what event in World War I tipped the balance against the Central Powers?

29. Why did the Germans want revenge?

30. List the nine governments that have been behind most of the worst wars since the Middle Ages.

31. What is the usual date and event cited as the start of World War II?

32. What date does Uncle Eric say marks the real beginning of World War II, and what event took place on that date?

33. What was the significance of the Spanish Civil War and when did it begin?

34. What was the main conflict of World War II?

35. What was the idea behind "appeasement" by the British and French governments when Germany took back the Rhineland?

36. When did Hitler formally declare an end to the Treaty of Versailles?

37. What was the Soviet-German Nonaggression Pact and when was it signed?

38. Who conquered more territory between 1919 and 1940, Berlin or Moscow?

39. The declaration of war by Britain and France meant what to their colonies around the world?

40. What is the Tripartite Pact and what deadly idea that leads to war is represented by it?

41. What was the European political philosophy that was popular for thousands of years and still popular in Europe when World War II broke out?

42. According to Uncle Eric, what two political philosophies were battling for supremacy over each other in World War II, and which won?

43. What is the significance of the Higgins boat?

44. Briefly, why should someone never invade Russia?

45. Who was the last person to successfully mount a winter invasion of Russia; how long did it take?

46. What is the Russian defensive strategy? Why?

47. When did the first snow fall after the German invasion of Russia?

48. When do most people believe the U.S. government entered World War II?

49. Why does Uncle Eric see the attack on Russia by Hitler as the solution to the war?

50. Uncle Eric says, "Knowing the events of World War II is important. Knowing the sequence is more important." Why is this important?

51. Who was the chief naval power in the Orient by the 1930s?

52. Why was the *Panay* incident significant? The *Panay* incident illustrates which of the deadly ideas that lead to war?

53. Why does Uncle Eric say it is unlikely that anyone would attack the United States or even provoke the United States to a fight unless they believed they had no alternative?

54. What was the Atlantic Charter?

55. What hidden agreement did Roosevelt make with Churchill that violated the U.S. Constitution?

56. Why are logistics important in a war?

57. In 1941 who was the chief supplier of oil, iron, and other necessary resources to Japan?

58. What was McCollum's eight-point plan intended to do?

59. What was significant about the Flying Tigers and who they worked for?

60. When did Admiral Kimmel warn Roosevelt about a possible attack on Pearl Harbor? What was the root cause for Kimmel's concern?

61. What is significant about the Prokofiev Seamount in November 1941?

62. From where did the Japanese launch their planes?

63. What is Executive Order No. 9066? On what date was it signed?

64. What percentage of the Japanese placed in U.S. concentration camps were United States citizens?

65. Why is the story of the Panzer Lehr Division important?

66. Who changed sides from the Axis to the Allies in 1943?

67. Who was fighting whom in the Pacific Theater?

68. Who was fighting whom in the European Theater?

69. What was the main battlefield of the war?

70. Where was the worst battle in history fought and how many died?

71. What was the biggest battle on the Western Front and how many died?

72. What was the single largest military operation in all of human history?

73. Strategically, could Hitler beat both Russia and Britain?

74. What is significant about Congresswoman Jeannette Rankin?

75. Uncle Eric says that once you understand the economics of World War II you would see what others do not. What does he mean?

76. What production mistake did Hitler make in World War II?

77. Why does Uncle Eric place so much emphasis on acquisition of oil in World War II?

78. What percentage of oil did the Allies control and what percent did the Axis control in World War II?

79. By 1944, what material was the German Heinkel 162 jet fighter mostly made of and why?

80. What did the June 1941 Brookings Institution report have to say about Germany's ability to produce weapons and supplies?

81. How did the German invasion of Russia differ from a normal invasion of a country?

82. What do most people think was the reason for the invasion of Normandy and what was the real purpose behind the invasion of Normandy?

83. What did the Moscow Declaration say?

84. When was the Battle of Stalingrad and what was significant about it?

85. When did Franklin Roosevelt call for Unconditional Surrender and what effect did Unconditional Surrender have on extending the war?

86. What was the one other historic case of Unconditional Surrender that Churchill's advisor, Lord Maurice Hankey, found? What happened to the loser?

87. Why didn't the Japanese surrender? What caused them to fight so fiercely, even when they knew they were defeated?

88. What is the reason cited by journalist Peter Wyden in his book DAY ONE, for the atomic bombing of Japan?

89. When did Truman halt Lend Lease aid to the USSR? Why is this date significant?

90. What was the result of World War I on the Russian people?

91. What political philosophy came into power as the result of the 1917 Russian Revolution?

92. What was Operation Keelhaul?

93. When did Soviet troops invade Afghanistan?

94. When did Soviet Empire begin to collapse?

95. Who emerged as the most powerful person in the Old World following World War II?

96. How much land did Stalin directly control following World War II?

97. What was the Truman Doctrine?

98. By the year 2000, how many countries did the U.S. sphere of influence include?

99. What is the root cause of terrorist attacks against the U.S.?

100. What are the two laws that make peace, liberty, and prosperity possible?

Answers

Uncle Eric's Model of How the World Works

Short Answer/Fill-in/True or False

1. Uncle Eric says that models are how we think. They are how we understand how the world works.

2. According to Uncle Eric, models are important because we constantly refer to our models to help us determine what incoming data is important and what data is not.

3. It is important to sort incoming data because we need to decide what incoming data we need to remember or file for future reference, and what data we can discard, based on its importance to us, or its usefulness. We need a tool for making this determination. That tool is also called our "model."

4. This answer requires the student to draw his/her own conclusion based on the information provided in the explanation of "Uncle Eric's Model of How the World Works." Possible answer: We should always be willing to test our models against incoming data, and if our models don't stand up to the incoming data, then it becomes necessary to question and perhaps rethink our model, as well as question the reliability of the incoming data.

5. Free market economics and Higher Law are the two models Uncle Eric thinks are most reliable, as well as crucially important for everyone to learn. Free market economics and Higher Law are important models because they show how human civilization works, especially the world of money.

6. **Fascism** is the political philosophy that is no philosophy at all. It embraces the concept that those in power can do whatever appears necessary to achieve their goals.

Discussion/Essay/Assignment

7. Examples of models will vary and might include scientific models, religious models, economic models, political models, etc.

8. The book WORLD WAR II explains how the U.S. government's involvement in the wars of Europe and Asia turned them into World Wars. By examining the wars through the eyes of Uncle Eric, readers have an opportunity to test the model they have previously used for studying the world wars to see if their model stands up to the economic, legal, and historical data presented through Uncle Eric's letters.

9. Answers will vary.

10. Look at the front matter of your dictionary. There should be an explanation of the "Order of Definitions." For example, the order of definitions can be historical order: the earliest meaning is placed first and later meanings are arranged by semantic development.

11. The reader must understand what the author means by the words the author uses so the reader can understand the progression of the author's ideas that build on the definition of the terms used. This does not require that a reader agree with the author's definition of a word, only that the reader understand what the author means when the author uses the word. Then the reader is in a better position to critically examine the author's ideas based on a common understanding of the author's meaning.

12. Answers will vary, but might include some of the following explanations: Definitions provide clear understanding and communication between the parties involved. For example, suppose you eat a piece of fruit. This fruit happens to be a banana. Someone comes along who has never before seen or tasted a banana. With the banana in your presence, you can each begin to discuss its merits, and you will each know exactly what you're talking about. As in the Richard Feynman example, you are understanding the characteristics of

the banana that go into making up what that "thing" is. To be able to give the "thing" a name, banana, that both parties can use in future communication will help promote speedier and clearer communication. This is the purpose of always making sure that you understand the definition of a term used in a discussion (whether in conversation or in books). You don't have to agree with the person's definition, but if you understand what the person means by it, you can have a clearer and more meaningful discussion instead of getting bogged down in misunderstandings regarding fuzzy language.

Author's Disclosure

Short Answer/Fill-in/True or False

1. Juris Naturalism is the belief in a Natural Law that is higher than any government's law.

Discussion/Essay/Assignment

2. Answers will vary, but students should note that the bias or philosophical slant of an author, news commentator, or reporter can influence the selection of facts included in a book or report, thereby slanting the history, or other subject areas.

3. Answers will vary.
4. Answers will vary.
5. Answers will vary.
6. Answers will vary.

Thought Exercises

Save the responses to all Thought Exercises. Students will be asked to revisit these questions and their answers.

1. Answers will vary, but should show thought and logic.
2. Answers will vary, but should show thought and logic.
3. Answers will vary, but should show thought and logic.

Cast of Characters

1. Answers will vary.

2. During WWII few women were in positions of power.

3. *Allies—World War II*   *Axis—World War II*
   (enemies of the Axis)   (enemies of the Allies)
      Great Britain   Germany
      United States   Italy
      Russia   Japan
                                           (also Bulgaria, Finland, Hungary, Romania)

Chapter 1: The Main Theater of the War

Define

1. Allies. Enemies of the Axis, led by Britain, United States, Russia.

2. Axis. Enemies of the Allies, led by Germany, Italy, Japan.

3. USSR. Union of Soviet Socialist Republics. The Russian Empire. Headquarters, the Kremlin in Moscow.

4. Eastern Front. The war in East Europe. Mostly involving Russia and Germany

Short Answer/Fill-In/True or False

5. Among the Allied Powers, the USSR suffered the greatest number of casualties: 18,000,000.

6. Among the Axis Powers, Germany suffered the greatest number of casualties: 4,200,000.

7. World War II was mainly a battle between Germany and the USSR.

8. Poland was caught between Germany and the USSR.

9. The Eastern Front was fought mainly in east Europe and mainly involved Russia and Germany.

10. More than 28 million were killed on the Eastern Front. This was 75% of all the deaths in the war.

11. The other major fronts of World War II included the Pacific Theater, Western Front, North Africa, the Italian Campaign, Southeast Asia, and the Balkans.

12. Answers will vary.

Activity

13. By completing this activity the student should better understand the loss of life suffered by those countries involved in World War II.

Chapter 2: Good Guys Against Bad Guys

Define

1. White hats against black hats. An expression from early western movies in which the good guys wore white hats and the bad guys wore black hats.

Short Answer/Fill-In/True or False

2. Uncle Eric believes government is about power—getting power and using it. The principles on which America was founded were about limiting government's power. Uncle Eric embraces America's founding principles, but not government.

3. USG refers to the United States government.

Chapter 3: Not Six Million

Define

1. Jewish Holocaust. The systematic murder of Jews by Hitler and his followers during World War II.

2. Genocide. The systematic killing of a whole national or ethnic group.

3. Labor camps. A prison camp in which the inmates are used as slave labor. Often inmates are worked to death.

4. Fascism. The political philosophy that is no philosophy at all. Do whatever appears necessary. It is derived from the law of the Roman Empire.

5. Socialism. An economic and political system under which virtually everything and everyone is owned and controlled by government agencies.

Short Answer/Fill-In/True or False

6. Besides the Jews, the Nazis also murdered prisoners of war, the aged, the sick, homosexuals, Slavs, Serbs, Czechs, Italians, Poles, Ukrainians, and many others including, of course, anyone they thought might be plotting against them.

7. Millions were murdered by the allies of Germany: by Romanians, Hungarians, Austrians, French, Croatians, and others.

8. Stalin murdered 42.7 million people.

9. Stalin's Order #270 said that all Soviet troops taken prisoner would be considered traitors and shot, and their wives would be sent to labor camps. In effect, Stalin made his whole army into a suicide army.

10. Hitler wanted to take over Europe, which totals 6.6 percent of the earth's land surface.

11. In keeping with the works of Lenin and Marx, Stalin wanted to conquer the world.

12. Marx's COMMUNIST MANIFESTO was written in 1848.

13. Gold was discovered at Sutter's Mill in California in January 1848.

14. In 1941 the U.S. government had only vague information about Hitler's death camps.

15. In 1941 the U.S. government knew that Stalin had murdered millions.

16. At the maximum extent of his reach, in 1942, Hitler controlled about 4 percent of the world.

17. The Soviet Socialists had conquered 16 percent of the world.

18. Britain had conquered 22 percent of the world.

19. The U.S.S.R. and China had murdered 52,886,000. Germany and Japan had murdered 26,910,000.

20. Uncle Eric believes the neutral Swiss were the good guys in World War II.

21. Before the Kremlin's empire collapsed in the 1990s, the Soviet Socialists murdered 61.9 million people.

Discussion/Essay/Assignment

22. Answers will vary.

23. Answers will vary

For Further Reading

24. Read THE OTHER VICTIMS.

Chapter 4: World War II Was Nothing New

Short Answer/Fill-In/True or False

1. Uncle Eric is attempting to show Chris that wars and death are not unusual events in the Old World. He also wants Chris to realize that historically speaking, Hitler was no more evil than many who went before him, as well as several of his contemporaries.

2. According to Uncle Eric, the Second World War was about the joy and abuse of power.

Discussion/Essay/Assignment

3. Answers will vary.

4. Answers will vary.

Chapter 5: Millions

Short Answer/Fill-In/True or False

1. President Franklin Roosevelt sided with China in World War II. The Chinese Kuomintang murdered 10,214,000; the Japanese regime murdered 5,964,000.

2. The Chinese people rebelled against the brutality of the Chinese Kuomintang.

3. The Red Chinese took over China in 1949.

4. Red means Socialist.

5. The Red Chinese murdered 35 million.

6. The Soviet Union was geographically closer to the United States by way of the Bering Strait, which was 55 miles from the U.S. territory of Alaska.

7. In terms of the number of people murdered and the geographical proximity, Stalin was the greater threat to the United States.

Chapter 6: Britain Was A White Hat?

Define

1. Blitz. The German bombing of England. The meaning is often restricted only to the German bombing of London in 1940.

Short Answer/Fill-In/True or False

2. By 1940, Britain had conquered 22% of the world.

3. "The sun never sets on the British Empire" meant that London held stolen territories around the globe so somewhere in the British Empire it was always daylight.

4. Outside Britain the government rarely obeyed the Old British Common Law.

5. Most of the deaths caused by Britain occurred in centuries prior to the 20th century.

6. Much of the British army and navy were not available for defense of Britain because it was scattered all over the world trying to hang onto all the nations London had conquered.

7. The question to ask is: "What right does America have to be involved in this foreign place?"

For Further Reading

8. Read chapters 40, 41, and 42 about the Treaty of Versailles in Richard Maybury's book WORLD WAR I.

Chapter 7: British Conquests

Short Answer/Fill-In/True or False

1. When history books are written by the victors, then history will generally be slanted in favor of the victors. The other side of the story, those who were defeated, will seldom be favorably told.

2. The British first invaded Ireland in 1170.

3. Ireland never invaded England.

4. Not likely. Child C and Child A are more likely to have a strained relationship with each other because of their relationship to Child B. In war, when Country A pledges allegiance to Country B, Country A is also pledging to stand against that country's enemies: Countries C, D, E, etc.

Chapter 8: P.T. Barnum Knew

Short Answer/Fill-In/True or False

1. The British people gave the world the system of the old British Common Law and the Industrial Revolution, which resulted in civilization as we know it today.

2. They are recommended because they are examples of the British conquest of other peoples and nations.

3. Answers will vary.

Chapter 9: British Area Bombing

Define

1. Area bombing. A British term from World War II. The bombing of civilian housing areas for the purpose of killing and terrorizing civilian men, women, and children. Done mostly by the British to Germans, but also done to some extent by Americans to Germans and to a greater extent by Americans to Japanese.

Short Answer/Fill-In/True or False

2. According to Uncle Eric, the British were fighting for liberty and justice for the British—and for British domination over millions of others.

Discussion/Essay/Assignment

3. Answers will vary.

4. Answers will vary.

Chapter 10: Two Questions

Short Answer/Fill-In/True or False

1. The camera made it very difficult for the British government to impose its heavy-handedness on its colonies. They did not want cameras photographing ruthless behavior.

2. The Anglo-Saxonists believed that the white British and Americans were natural allies, superior to others, and entitled to rule the world.

Chapter 11: When Did the War Begin?

Define

1. Blitzkrieg. Lightning war. A German term meaning a swift, powerful strike spearheaded by tanks and aircraft.

Short Answer/Fill-In/True or False

2. In 1917 President Wilson abandoned neutrality and joined the Allies, which caused victory for the Allies.

3. The Germans wanted revenge because the Treaty of Versailles so impoverished them that they were desperate to escape their situation.

4. The nine governments that have been behind most of the worst wars since the Middle Ages are: Beijing, Berlin, London, Moscow, Paris, Rome, Tokyo, Vienna, and Washington D.C.

5. By the 1930s the Allies were comprised of London, Paris, and Moscow (Britain, France, and Russia); they were an older group than the Axis.

6. By the 1930s the Axis were comprised of Rome, Tokyo, and Berlin (Italy, Japan, and Germany).

7. The only way for the younger members of the Usual Suspects to expand their empires was to steal from the older members of the Usual Suspects what Britain, France, and Russia had already stolen.

8. The Germans invaded Poland on September 1, 1939.

9. Uncle Eric says that the invasion of Manchuria by Japan in 1931 marks the real beginning of World War II.

10. The Spanish Civil War, which began in July 1936, was a preview of the conflict between fascism and socialism that would eventually be played out between Germany and Russia on the Eastern Front.

11. The main event of World War II was the Eastern Front, a conflict between Germany and Russia.

12. The Eastern Front was a battle between two forms of tyranny: fascism (Germany) and socialism (Russia).

13. The U.S. government sided with Russia and socialism.

For Research

14. Answers may vary.

For Further Reading

15. Read FRIEDRICH by Hans Peter Richter.

Chapter 12: Appeasement and Comparative Brutality

Short Answer/Fill-In/True or False

1. "Appeasement" was the idea that if the German Nazis and Italian fascists were allowed to take a small amount of territory, then they would be satisfied and would not try to take huge amounts of territory, as the governments of Britain, France, and Russia had done for centuries.

2. The main reason Britain and France were vulnerable to Germany was that Britain and France had their armies, navies, and air forces scattered all over the world controlling the people they had conquered.

3. In 2002, the U.S. government had troops stationed in more than 100 countries.

Chapter 13: Carving Up Central Europe

Define

1. Mobilize. To prepare for war. To arm troops and move them near expected areas of fighting.

Short Answer/Fill-In/True or False

2. In 1937 Hitler formally declared an end to the Treaty of Versailles.

3. Germany annexed Austria in 1938.

4. In October 1938, Hitler's troops invaded the Sudetenland.

5. Besides Germany, the countries of Britain, Poland, and Hungary also grabbed parts of Czechoslovakia in 1938.

6. In August 1939, Berlin and Moscow agreed to the Soviet-German Nonaggression Pact in which Hitler and Stalin agreed not to attack each other. This also said that Berlin would get a large part of Poland for its new empire, and Moscow could have the rest of Poland, plus Finland, Estonia, Latvia, and Lithuania.

7. The Hollywood version of history says Hitler's September 1, 1939 attack on Poland was the trigger for war, and the Axis powers were the bad guys and the Allies were the good guys.

8. Only 16 days after Hitler's attack, Poland was also invaded by Stalin, a member of the Allies. On November 30, 1939, Stalin attacked Finland. On June 17, 1940, Stalin invaded and conquered Latvia, Lithuania, and Estonia.

9. Moscow conquered more territory between 1919 and 1940 than did Berlin.

10. The British and French did nothing after the Soviets invaded Poland.

11. This meant all the British and French colonies around the world would again find themselves at war with the Germans.

12. On June 10, 1940, Italy came into the war on the side of Berlin.

13. In September 1940, Rome, Berlin, and Tokyo signed the Tripartite Pact in which they agreed that if one of them went to war with someone, they all would.

14. Alliances is the deadly idea represented by the Tripartite Pact. Rome, Berlin, and Tokyo agreed that if one got into a war, they all would come to the defense of the other, which escalated the war into a world war.

Chapter 14: The French versus the French

Short Answer/Fill-In/True or False

1. The main point of Uncle Eric's letter about "The French versus the French" is that the Hollywood version of the war is wrong. All of France was not anti-German and pro-Ally. Some of the French were anti-German and others were pro-Ally. Northern France was "Free France" or "Occupied France" and was pro-Ally. Southern France, or "Vichy France" was pro-Germany. The pro-Axis French actually fought the Allies, as well as their own French people who were for the Allies. The same scenario occurred in Austria and Czechoslovakia.

2. In North Africa the Usual Suspects were fighting over stolen land. The U.S. troops fought against the French and the Germans, battling to decide the ownership of North Africa, which is Arab. It was the Usual Suspects battling to decide the ownership of the stolen land–North Africa.

3. Fascism was the European political philosophy that was popular for thousands of years and still popular in Europe when World War II broke out.

4. World War II was mostly a battle between fascists and socialists, and with the USG's help, the socialists won.

Chapter 15: Significance of the Higgins Boat

Short Answer/Fill-In/True or False

1. The Higgins boat was invented in the U.S. to land troops and equipment on beaches. The Germans had none. As a result the Germans had to capture a port to land troops and equipment. Because they were unable to invade Britain by boat, the Germans had to resort to an air war known as the Battle of Britain.

2. The Battle of Britain ended on October 31, 1940.

3. The Japanese attacked Pearl Harbor on December 7, 1941.

4. After the Battle of Britain, Hitler invaded the Soviet Union on June 22, 1941.

Chapter 16: Only Genghis Khan Did It

Short Answer/Fill-In/True or False

1. Russia is too big, too cold, too wet, and too flat to successfully invade. The only months available for fighting a full-scale war are the three summer months.

2. The last person to mount a successful winter invasion of Russia was Genghis Khan in 1236 AD, and it took him four years.

3. The Russian defensive strategy is to keep retreating until winter arrives. The enemy must then confront severe weather and fragile supply lines. When the snow melts, the Russians cut the supply lines and attack.

4. After the German invasion of Russia, the first snow fell in Russia on September 12, 1941.

5. In June 1941, the Germans took a half-million vehicles into Russia. By November, only 75,000 were still working.

6. Uncle Eric says that September 12, 1941 is the most important date of World War II because the snow began falling in Russia and, as a result, Germany became unable to conquer Russia. The war was winding down.

7. The U.S. government entered the war on December 7, 1941.

Chapter 17: The Solution

Short Answer/Fill-In/True or False

1. Uncle Eric believes that if Hitler and Stalin fought each other, they would so weaken each other that neither would emerge a threat to the rest of the world for some time to come.

2. According to Uncle Eric, "America's entry into the war on December 7th was not needed because the German war machine was already in deep trouble on September 12th, when the first snow fell in Russia."   Knowing the sequence of events demonstrates that many of the history lessons that teach about the necessity of the United States joining World War II are wrong. The war was ending without U.S. involvement.

Chapter 18: Events Leading to Pearl Harbor

Short Answer/Fill-In/True or False

1. Japan was the chief naval power in the Orient by the 1930s.

2. Tokyo wanted all conquering Europeans out of the Orient, and then wanted to control the Orient.

3. In 1937 a group of U.S. navy ships led by the gunboat Panay was escorting merchant ships on the Yangtze River in China, which was a war zone, when Japanese planes attacked the group, sinking the Panay, three oil supply vessels, and killing three people.

4. The Panay incident illustrates these two deadly ideas that lead to war: global protection and interests.

5. The Panay incident was significant because the USG was involved in this incident in China, yet Japan was sending a clear message to the USG to get out of China. The Panay incident in 1937 marked the entry of America into World War II.

6. Yes, Franklin Roosevelt did violate the Neutrality Act by sending U.S. armed forces to China to protect people who had taken the risk of entering a war zone.

Chapter 19: Hiding Facts about the Brawl

Short Answer/Fill-In/True or False

1. Uncle Eric says the United States was the undisputed industrial giant of the world, more powerful in economic and military terms than any other nation. Also, the Axis only controlled 3.3% of the earth's land surface while the British had conquered 22% and the Russians 16%. It didn't make economic sense that the Axis could outfight the United States or the Allies.

2. Formerly secret documents were revealed under the 1966 Freedom of Information Act that made new information available.

Discussion/Essay/Assignment

3. Answers will vary.

Chapter 20: The Great World War II Myth

Short Answer/Fill-In/True or False

1. Answers will vary.
2. Answers will vary.

For Research

3. Answers will vary.

Chapter 21: A Secret Agreement

Short Answer/Fill-In/True or False

1. The Atlantic Charter was a loosely worded agreement for the governments of Britain and the U.S. to work together toward peace, economic advancement, freedom of travel, and "general security."

2. Roosevelt agreed to commit American forces to a war, even if Japan attacked British, not United States, territory. The agreement, which was hidden, was not approved by Congress, which is required by the U.S. Constitution. It also violated the Neutrality Act.

3. Roosevelt had promised the American people, "Your boys are not going to be sent into any foreign wars."

4. Churchill told Roosevelt, "Were I to become Prime Minister of Britain we could control the world."

5. In 1939 Britain controlled 22% of the world.

Chapter 22: Why did the Japanese Attack?

Define

1. Logistics. The ability to supply the troops with bullets, food, hardware, etc.

Short Answer/Fill-In/True or False

2. Logistics are important in a war because the side with the ability to move quickly and transport the most supplies to the battlefield would be the winner.

3. In 1941, the chief supplier of oil, iron, and other necessary resources to Japan was the United States.

4. Answers will vary.

Discussion/Essay/Assignment

5. Answers will vary.
6. Answers will vary.

Chapter 23: Pearl Harbor, FDR's Deceit

Define

1. Freeze. To hold assets and prevent the owner from having access to them.

2. Expeditionary force. A military force whose job is not defensive, but offensive. To leave the country and fight abroad.

Short Answer/Fill-In/True or False

3. In 1940, 88% percent of Americans opposed the U.S. getting involved in the war.

4. Lieutenant Commander Arthur H. McCollum was placed in charge of all intelligence information about Japan that was routed to President Roosevelt.

5. McCollum believed the U.S. should get into the war to help Britain defeat Germany.

6. McCollum's eight-point plan was intended to provoke Japan into committing an overt act of war against the U.S. He believed this would then change the minds of the American people about getting involved in the war.

7. No, every step in McCollum's Eight-Point Plan was executed by one or more events.

8. McCollum's Eight-Point Plan, executed.

    Step 1: Get permission from the British to put U.S. ships in Britain's Pacific bases, especially Singapore (near the oil fields of the Dutch East Indies, which are now called Indonesia).
    > 4 October 1940. Churchill gives permission to put U.S. warships in Singapore, which is near the oil fields of the Dutch East Indies (Indonesia).

    Step 2: Get permission from the Dutch to put U.S. ships in the Dutch East Indies.
    > 13 November 1940. The Dutch give permission to base U.S. warships in the Dutch East Indies (Indonesia).

    Step 3: Give all possible aid to the Chinese government, led by Chiang Kai-Shek, against Japan.
    > 11 March 1941. Congress passes FDR's "Lend-Lease act," which gives money and other resources to the governments of Britain and China to fight the Japanese. (Three months later, U.S. aid will go to Stalin and anyone else who will fight Japan or Germany.)

    > August 1941. FDR has illegally given permission for creation of the Flying Tigers to help Chiang Kai-Shek fight the Japanese in China.

    Step 4: Send heavy cruisers to the Orient.
    > 15 March 1941. FDR begins secretly sending cruisers and destroyers into Japanese home waters.

    Step 5: Send submarines to the Orient.
    > 1 January 1941. Twenty-four U.S. submarines have been sent to the Orient.

    Step 6: Move the U.S. fleet from San Diego to Hawaii.
    > April 1940. FDR begins moving the Pacific fleet from San Diego to Pearl Harbor.

    Step 7: Ask the Dutch to cut off supplies of oil to Japan.
    > 13 November 1940. Under pressure from FDR, the Dutch reduce their supply of oil to Japan.

Step 8: Cut off U.S. and British supplies of oil and all other supplies to Japan.
>   25 July 1940. FDR reduces the supply of oil and metals to Japan.
>   26 September 1940. FDR cuts off the supply of iron to Japan.
>   26 July 1941. FDR freezes all Japanese assets; reduces Japanese oil supply by 90%.

9.   Snow had fallen in Russia on September 12, 1941 turning the war in favor of the Allies. Germany could not withstand a Russian winter. This is significant because there was no need for the U.S. to get involved in the war. It was going to end.

10. Answers will vary.

Chapter 24: The Flying Tigers and B-17 Bombers

Short Answer/Fill-In/True or False

1.   The official name of the Flying Tigers was the American Volunteers Group.

2.   Officially, the Flying Tigers were independent volunteers hired and financed by the Chinese government to fight the Japanese, months before the attack on Pearl Harbor.

3.   The Flying Tigers were secretly created and financed by the U.S. government for the purpose of fighting the Japanese.

4.   By starting the Flying Tigers, FDR had declared war on the Japanese before the Japanese had attacked Pearl Harbor.

5.   The entire factory production of the B-17 Flying Fortress was located in the Philippines where, according to Uncle Eric, their only conceivable targets could be the Japanese.

To View

6.   THE FLYING TIGERS (1942) starring John Wayne.
7.   THIRTEEN DAYS (2000) starring Kevin Costner.

Chapter 25: "Caught With Their Pants Down"

Short Answer/Fill-In/True or False

1.   On June 9, 1941, Admiral Kimmel met with Roosevelt to tell him about a possible Japanese attack on Pearl Harbor.

2.   Kimmel was concerned because he didn't have enough planes or anti-aircraft guns to protect the fleet.

3.   No, Roosevelt gave Kimmel no additional planes or anti-aircraft guns, nor did Roosevelt return the ships, planes, and guns he had taken away in May.

4.   Kimmel got all guns firing within seven minutes of the beginning of the Japanese attack on Pearl Harbor.

5.   The Japanese were able to cause so much damage because Kimmel had been left with too few guns and planes to protect the fleet.

Discussion/Essay/Assignment

6.   Answers will vary.

Chapter 26: Planes Parked Too Close Together

Short Answer/Fill-In/True or False

1.   A commander guards against air attack by scattering his planes widely apart in camouflaged spots.

2.   A commander guards against sabotage and espionage by parking planes close together in well-lighted areas so guards can better protect them.

3.   Kimmel and Short received no information about the Japanese fleet heading for Pearl Harbor. Without that information they believed they were more vulnerable to sabotage and espionage than an air attack.

4.   Forty percent of the population of Hawaii was of Japanese descent.

Discussion/Essay/Assignment

5.   Answers will vary.

Chapter 27: The Prokofiev Seamount

Short Answer/Fill-In/True or False

1.   In anticipation of a possible Japanese attack, Admiral Kimmel sent his fleet to the Prokofiev Seamount to thwart any possible attack, which Kimmel believed would happen from that location. But the USG ordered Kimmel and his fleet back to Pearl Harbor.

2.   Kimmel had been ordered to send his modern ships away from Pearl Harbor.

3.   The Arizona had eight anti-aircraft guns; the Washington had 87.

4.   The Japanese launched their planes from the Prokofiev Seamount.

Chapter 28: The Necessary Sacrifice?

Short Answer/Fill-In/True or False

1.   The "Necessary Sacrifice" explanation says that a plan was made to bait the Japanese into attacking Pearl Harbor, and the sacrifice of soldiers and equipment was necessary to change American opinion to join the war to stop Germany from taking over the world.

2.   The error in reasoning is that it was unnecessary to join the war because with Hitler in Russia during the winter, the war was coming to an end, without the U.S. needing to get involved.

3.   Executive Order No. 9066 was signed on February 19, 1942, and required U.S. Army troops to round up persons of Japanese ancestry.

4. Seventy percent of the Japanese placed in U.S. concentration camps were United States citizens.

5. No, placing Japanese in U.S. concentration camps was a complete violation of the U.S. Constitution.

6. No government official was ever prosecuted for internment of the Japanese.

Discussion/Essay/Assignment

7. Answers will vary.

8. Answers will vary.

For Further Reading

9. Read Roy Uyeda's story.

10. Read JOURNEY TO TOPAZ by Yoshiko Uchida.

11. Read FAREWELL TO MANZANAR by Jeanne Wakatsuki Houston & James D. Houston.

Chapter 29: You've Seen the Photos

Short Answer/Fill-In/True or False

1. The Arizona exploded 12 minutes after the attack on Pearl Harbor.

2. Answers will vary.

Chapter 30: The Myth of German Might

Define

1. Napalm. Jellied gasoline that erupts in an inferno when it hits the ground.

Short Answer/Fill-In/True or False

2. The Hollywood version of history says that Hitler, with his superior German technology, could have taken over the world if not stopped.

3. The economics of war studies the production and distribution of goods and services of war.

4. The story of the Panzer Lehr Division is important because even though the Panzer Lehr tanks were superior to the American Sherman tanks the 45 Panzer Lehr tanks were no match against 2000 Allied planes. And the most important part of the story is that the German government was unable to produce many replacements. So, even though the technology was superior, the Germans couldn't reproduce that technology.

5. Italy changed sides in 1943, joining the Allies.

Chapter 31: Focus on the Eastern Front

Define

1. Division. Generally, six brigades. An infantry division is about 10,000 troops. An armored division, about 600 tanks. Typically, but not always, there are nine troops in a squad, three squads to a platoon, four platoons to a company, six companies to a battalion, two battalions to a brigade, and six brigades to a division.

Short Answer/Fill-In/True or False

2. In the Pacific Theater the war was primarily the U.S. versus Japan.

3. The European Theater had two main fronts: The Western Front and Eastern Front.

    a. The Western Front was mainly Britain, parts of France, and later the U.S., against Germany.

    b. The Eastern Front was Germany versus the USSR.

       (NOTE: The European Theater also included the Italian Campaign in Italy and other minor conflicts, like the Balkans.)

4. The main battlefield of the war was the Eastern Front, between Hitler and Stalin.

5. The Battle at Stalingrad (now Volgograd) on the Eastern Front was the worst in all of human history. It lasted five months and killed 1,110,000.

6. The biggest battle on the Western Front was the D-Day landings on the Normandy beaches. Except for small pockets of resistance, that battle was over in 72 hours. Deaths of Allied troops numbered less than 2,500. German and civilian deaths are unknown but were probably not more than 10,000.

7. The Western Front battle had 12,500 deaths versus 1,110,000 on the Eastern Front.

8. Hitler's attack on Stalin in June 1941 was the single largest military operation in all of human history. Of the Wehrmacht's 209 divisions, Hitler used 144 to attack the Soviet Union.

Chapter 32: Of Photographs and Weather

For Discussion and Research

1. Answers will vary.

To View

2. ENEMY AT THE GATES. Rated R. Parental discretion advised.

Chapter 33: German Production of Weapons

Define

1. Strategic. Planning, maneuver, and placement of forces — not what the forces are, but where they are and how they are used.

Short Answer/Fill-In/True or False

2. Germany excelled at the beginning of the war because they had been gearing up for war for years. The Allied countries were behind the Germans in war production at the start of the war. Additionally, Germany's generals were brilliant compared to the generals of the Allied governments.

3. Germany was producing not even a 1/3 of the combined weaponry of Britain and the USSR.

4. Germany had 66 million people. Britain had 46 million and the Soviet Union had 166 million. Britain and the USSR were allies so their total populations were 232 million compared to Germany's 66 million.

5. Another 500 million people comprised the British colonies.

6. Hitler attacked Stalin on June 22, 1941.

7. Hitler could not beat both Russia and Britain. Britain's navy was superior to Hitler's and the Russian artillery was greater than Hitler's; also Hitler was going to fight on Russian soil, during a Russian winter.

8. Jeannette Rankin was the only member of Congress who voted against declaring war on the Axis. She also voted against participation in World War I and led protest marches against the Vietnam War.

9. The significant point is that Germany was outmanned and outproduced by the Allies, even before the U.S. government became involved. It was unnecessary for the U.S. government to join the war.

For Research

10. Essays will vary.

Chapter 34: Germany's Unknown Second Army

Short Answer/Fill-In/True or False

1. Germany had the small high-tech mechanized army, as well as the main body of the army, which were foot soldiers and horses.

2. Hitler had 3,350 tanks and Stalin had 15,000. Hitler had 650,000 horses.

3. Russia's generals were incompetent, while Germany's generals were brilliant.

4. If you look at the production side of the war, Germany was clearly outclassed. Economically, Hitler could not win.

Chapter 35: Tank Treads, Trucks, and Submarines

Short Answer/Fill-In/True or False

1. The treads on German tanks were narrow and designed to operate in non-arctic weather, on roads, and for speed. On Russian soil the German tanks sank in the mud and snow and became immobile. They were easy targets for the enemy.

2. Hitler opted for quality rather than quantity in World War II, as well as frequent design changes. German quality was great but they couldn't produce enough. Also, the frequent design changes meant they weren't producing enough parts to repair the myriad types of vehicles they were using.

3. Only 12 percent of Hitler's tank division was running in November 1941.

4. The weakness of Panzer I and Panzer II tanks was their limited amount of metal and gun size. They were training tanks, not meant for combat.

5. The first Tiger tank was so complicated and needed so many spare parts that it could only be repaired by putting it on a train and shipping it back to repair factories in Germany, a distance of up to 2,000 miles.

6. Germany's big tanks and performance aircraft were limited in number and did not work well. The Germans were outnumbered by the Allies, even before the U.S. entered the war.

Chapter 36: Germany's Wonder Weapons

Define

1. Prototype. An early experimental or demonstration version, not a mass production version. Usually, prototypes are made by hand.

Short Answer/Fill-In/True or False

2. The other side of the story is that these advancements were not a strength. They were a weakness. German factories were constantly having to shut down and retool for new designs, thus limiting the number that could be produced.

3. Hitler was constantly interfering with his engineers and insisting they make design changes.

Chapter 37: Oil and Rifles

Short Answer/Fill-In/True or False

1. Without oil, tanks don't run, planes don't fly, and ships don't sail.

2. The Allies had 90 percent of the oil and the Axis had 3 percent.

3. The Japanese had the Zero, a fighter plane, which was its only superior weapon early in the war. The U.S. fighters soon outclassed the Zero. Other weaponry by the Italians and Japanese were inferior to those of the Allies.

4. Germany was primarily a land power. Its navy was small and sunk early in the war.

Chapter 38: Americans Were Less Intelligent?

Short Answer/Fill-In/True or False

1. The P-51 is generally regarded as the finest propeller-driven aircraft to come out of World War II. It took 121 days from design to placing the first in the air; 15,686 were built.

2. Henry Ford built the B-24 starting in March 1941 in Willow Run, Michigan. The Willow Run plant assembly line was more than a mile long. The main assembly building covered 67 acres, and the total site was 900 acres. A four-engine B-24 contained 1.5 million parts. Henry Ford's Willow Run plant turned out one B-24 every 63 minutes. A total of 18,188 B-24 Liberators were built at all aircraft plants.

3. The Germans were able to put up 200 heavy bombers compared to America's 34,887 heavy bombers, plus 13,512 four-engine British Halifax and Lancaster heavy bombers. That was 200 against 48,399.

4. The Japanese had four Nakajima G8N Renzans.

5. By 1944 Germany was so short of aluminum and other metals that the new Heinkel 162 jet fighter had to be made mostly of wood.

6. America was outproducing the Axis by slightly less than 2 to 1 on aircraft and tanks and six times the artillery.

7. The Liberty ship was the main cargo ship of WWII. Henry J. Kaiser could build a Liberty ship in eight days. A total of 2,751 Liberty ships were built.

8. America built 146 aircraft carriers. Germany built one.

Chapter 39: The Brookings Revelation

Short Answer/Fill-In/True or False

1. The Brookings Institution reported that Germany, Italy, and their allies were short of lead, copper, cobalt, and most other industrial raw materials needed to make and operate weapons, as well as being short of food.

2. The report was published five months before the U.S. entered the war. This meant the U.S. had knowledge that the Axis Powers were in trouble. There was little reason for the U.S. to enter the war.

3. A key reason the Third Reich lost the war was because they ran out of fuel.

Chapter 40: Russia Invaded by Keystone Kops

Short Answer/Fill-In/True or False

1. Logistics is the ability to transport weaponry, food, and other supplies to the troops. The outcomes of nearly all wars are determined by logistics; the first side to run out of supplies loses.

2. Russia had made their railroad tracks a different gauge than those used in Western Europe.

3. The Germans had to move their logistics troops first to get the transportation route in place so they could then move their tanks, planes, and infantry. Usually it is the other way around.

4. The Eastern Front was 75% of the war so when the Germans failed in Russia in 1941, they ruined their entire war effort.

Chapter 41: Omaha Beach, Bravery vs. Heroism

Define

1. Berlin Wall. The wall between West Berlin and East Berlin erected in 1961 by the Kremlin. The wall was designed to keep Germans in Soviet-controlled East Germany from escaping to the West. The Berlin Wall became a symbol of Soviet tyranny, and when it was torn down in 1989, this triggered a domino effect that led to the collapse of the entire Soviet Empire.

Short Answer/Fill-In/True or False

2. D-Day was June 6, 1944.

3. Most people believe the invasion of Normandy was to liberate France and the rest of Western Europe from the Germans.

4. The real purpose for the invasion of Normandy was to open a second front to help Stalin who wanted German troops drawn away from the Eastern Front.

5. Because the U.S. aided Stalin and invaded Normandy, the USSR became a tyrannical superpower until the fall of the Berlin Wall in 1989. If the U.S. had not helped Stalin, both Germany and the USSR might have pummeled each other to a state of weakness in which neither would have emerged as a world threat.

Chapter 42: The German Underground

Short Answer/Fill-In/True or False

1. In the 1932 election Hitler received 42% of the votes.

2. The Hollywood version says that the invasion liberated France, however, many of the French were not members of the Allies; they chose to side with the Axis, so those who sided with the Axis were conquered, not liberated.

3. Yes, Germans tried to murder Hitler several times (there are 40 known attempts).

4. Yes, the German resistance did contact the Allies, but were refused assistance.

5. The German people were afraid of another treaty following WWII, like the Treaty of Versailles, that would blame the German people for everything and place financial burdens on them that would throw them into poverty, like the post World War I period.

6. General Rommel was involved in the attempt to assassinate Hitler on July 20, 1944, and afterward he was forced to commit suicide.

For Further Reading

7. HITLER'S GERMAN ENEMIES by Louis L. Snyder.

Chapter 43: Unconditional Surrender

Short Answer/Fill-In/True or False

1. The Moscow Declaration said that the Germans would be forced to pay reparations for the war again, which was just what the German people feared might happen.

2. The Battle of Stalingrad took place in September 1942 and was the worst battle in all of human history, killing 1.1 million people in five months. At the conclusion of the battle, Germany was losing the war.

3. Franklin Roosevelt called for Unconditional Surrender on January 24, 1943, one week before the Battle of Stalingrad ended.

4. Surrenders are usually conditional, meaning the losers agree to surrender so long as they are not harmed. Unconditional surrender means no guarantees for the losers. They can be killed. It usually causes an enemy to fight to the death, on the hope of victory; as they believe there is certain death if they surrender.

5. In an Unconditional Surrender the enemy becomes unwilling to surrender because the results can mean death.

6. Roosevelt announced his demand for Unconditional Surrender in January 1943. The war continued for two more years with men, women, and children dying at the rate of a million a month.

7. Of the three million German prisoners of war that were sent to Russia, half were never seen again.

8. The other historic case of Unconditional Surrender found by Lord Maurice Hankey was the war between the Romans and the Carthaginians. The Romans entirely destroyed Carthage.

9. The anti-Nazis needed a conditional surrender so that Germany would be protected from Stalin. Without the promise of protection, Stalin would most likely have taken over Germany and annihilated millions of people.

For Research

10. Research will vary.

Chapter 44: Why Did Roosevelt Do It?

Short Answer/Fill-In/True or False

1. Uncle Eric says that no one will ever know the reason why Roosevelt made the choices he did, but Uncle Eric's belief is that FDR prolonged the war in an effort to weaken all rivals, so the United States would emerge the strongest nation on earth.

2. Yes, Harry Truman maintained the demand for Unconditional Surrender.

Chapter 45: Rarely Questioned

Short Answer/Fill-In/True or False

1. The Ten Deadly Ideas that lead to war are: the Pax Romana, fascism, love of political power, global protection, interests, cost externalization, Manifest Destiny, alliances, the glory of war, and the White Man's Burden.

2. The Ten Deadly Ideas are the main reasons the U.S. government got into the two world wars and continues to get involved in world conflicts today.

Chapter 46: Why Was Nagasaki Bombed?

Short Answer/Fill-In/True or False

1. The Hollywood and U.S. government versions contain the following two assumptions about the end of WWII are:

    a. Dropping atomic bombs on Hiroshima and Nagasaki was necessary because the only other way to defeat Japan was an invasion that could have cost a million American lives.

    b. The Hiroshima bomb was the more important of the two.

2. The non-statist side says that both atomic bombings were unnecessary.

3. The bomb was dropped on Nagasaki on August 9, 1945, seventy-five hours after the atomic bomb was dropped on Hiroshima. On August 8, 1945, Hirohito and Togo were going to ask the Japanese War Council to announce Japan's surrender.

Chapter 47: 105 Aircraft Carriers

Short Answer/Fill-In/True or False

1. There was no need to bomb Japan with atomic bombs. They were close to surrender as it was. And there was no need to invade, either. With no natural resources and cut off from the rest of the world, Japan would eventually starve itself into the need to surrender or live in the Stone Age.

2. The U.S. government used area bombing on the Japanese. They dropped incendiary bombs to burn Japanese homes and cities, at the rate of one per day by August 1945.

Chapter 48: Surrender Near

For Discussion

1. Answers will vary.

Chapter 49: Fierce Fighters

Define

1. Cold War. The half-century standoff between Moscow and its allies, and Washington and its allies.

Short Answer/Fill-In/True or False

2. The Japanese were given the same terms for surrender as the Germans–Unconditional Surrender.

3. In DAY ONE, Peter Wyden states that the atomic bomb was dropped on Japan as a demonstration to frighten the Russians.

4. Truman halted Lend Lease aid to the USSR on May 12, 1945. The date is significant because it marked the beginning of the Cold War.

5. The atomic bomb was dropped on Nagasaki so quickly because the U.S. government used it to frighten the Russians, and they needed to drop it before Japan surrendered.

Chapter 50: The Russians React

Short Answer/Fill-In/True or False

1. The Russian people were given modern weapons to fight the Germans in World War I. Instead, they used the weapons on the Czar who was overthrown and killed. It was the 1917 Russian Revolution.

2. The socialists came into power following the 1917 Russian Revolution.

3. The "wreckers" were individuals who refused to follow the new socialist government's Five-Year Plan, and they were murdered.

Chapter 51: The Soviet Uprising

Short Answer/Fill-In/True or False

1. The reasons are not factually known. Only two assumptions were drawn by Uncle Eric: 1) The Russian people were frightened by the U.S. government's demonstration of the atomic bomb on Japan and believed the Soviet government was all that protected them from the U.S. 2) The Russian people were frightened and believed that if they fought with the Germans against the Allies that they could find no safe harbor and would be forcibly returned to the Soviet government if they were taken prisoner, which would result in almost certain death.

2. Operation Keelhaul was the program by which the Allies returned two million captured Soviet rebels in German uniforms to the Soviet government toward the end of the war to be executed or imprisoned.

3. Soviet troops invaded Afghanistan in 1979.

4. The Soviet Empire began to collapse in November 1989 with the tearing down of the Berlin Wall, about nine months after the Soviets fled Afghanistan.

Chapter 52: Arm Any Gangster

Short Answer/Fill-In/True or False

1. Joseph Stalin emerged as the most powerful person in the Old World following World War II.

2. Following World War II, Stalin directly controlled a sixth of all the land on earth.

3. The 1947 Truman Doctrine allowed the U.S. government to give money, weapons, and military training to anyone who claimed to be anti-Soviet. It stayed in effect until the collapse of the Soviet Empire in the 1990s.

4. At the time this book was written, the U.S. government provided money, military training, or other assistance to more than 100 governments.

5. Not more than 20 governments are limited enough that an American would feel comfortable living in them without being able to get out safely.

6. In an attempt to prevent the rise of another Hitler, the U.S. government formed alliances with anyone who claimed to be anti-Soviet and pro-American.

7. By the year 2000, the U.S. sphere of influence comprised more than 100 countries, the largest empire the world has ever known.

8. The root cause of terrorist attacks against the U.S. is revenge against the U.S. from the victims of U.S. backed countries.

For Research

9. Papers will vary.

Chapter 53: September 11th

Discussion/Essay/Assignment

1. Answers will vary.
2. Answers will vary.
3. Answers will vary.

For Research

4. Reports will vary.

For Further Reading

5. THE THOUSAND YEAR WAR IN THE MIDEAST: HOW IT AFFECTS YOU TODAY, by Richard J. Maybury, published by Bluestocking Press, web site: www.BluestockingPress.com

---

Chapter 54: Blowback

Define

1. Blowback. A Central Intelligence Agency term, means retaliation by victims of Washington's foreign interventions.

For Research and Discussion

2. Research will vary.

Chapter 55: MAD

Define

1. MAD. Mutually Assured Destruction. Nuclear policy of Washington and the Kremlin.

Short Answer/Fill-In/True or False

2. The H-bomb was detonated in 1961 and was 2,500 times as powerful as the A-bomb that destroyed Hiroshima.

To View

3. THIRTEEN DAYS (2000) starring Kevin Costner.

Chapter 56: Police Officers of the World

Define

1.   No-fly zone. An area where one power forbids another power to fly its planes.

Short Answer/Fill-In/True or False

2.   Briefly, Washington wanted Americans to visit foreign countries and trade with foreign countries, but he did not want Americans to get involved in their politics or their wars. He wanted the U.S. to remain politically neutral.

3.   The two laws that make peace, liberty, and prosperity possible are: 1) Do all you have agreed to do (this is the basis of contract law), and 2) do not encroach on other persons or their property (this is the basis of tort law and some criminal law).

Discussion/Essay/Assignment

4.   Essays will vary.

5.   Answers will vary.

6.   A family can begin to develop its own case law through this exercise.

Chapter 57: Summary

Discussion/Essay/Assignment

1.   World War II was a battle of good versus evil, and good barely triumphed. To prevent another such catastrophe, the U.S. must have military forces that are global police officers, ready to go to any corner of the globe to fight evil.

2.   The U.S. government gave aid to the USSR during WWII, which made their enemies our enemies and spawned the terrorism we face in America today.

3.   Answers will vary.

Chapter 58: The Needless Deaths of 35 Million

Discussion/Essay/Assignment

1.   Answers will vary.

2.   Answers will vary.

Chapter 59: The Normal Condition of Humans

Define

1.   Fungible. Transportable and of uniform characteristics, so that one unit of the item can substitute for any other unit, as one gallon of pure water can substitute for any other gallon of pure water.

Short Answer/Fill-In/True or False

2.   Foreign aid sent as food, clothing, medicine, etc. frees up monies the foreign country would have used for these purposes, so they can now use those monies for weapons.

Chapter 60: The Cause of War

Short Answer/Fill-In/True or False

1.   According to Uncle Eric, the world wars were about political power.

Chapter 61: Minor League to Emperor of the World

Short Answer/Fill-In/True or False

1.   Uncle Eric thinks the rest of the story about the World Wars is not widely known for two reasons: 1) Most Americans do not distinguish between their government and their country. So if their government does something evil, then they, too, are culpable. 2) Franklin Roosevelt is widely regarded as one of America's greatest Presidents. If he is responsible for so many bad mistakes, then many Americans will think no President can be trusted.

2.   Uncle Eric wants America to remain neutral in foreign policy.

Thought Exercises Revisited

1. Answers will vary.

2. Answers will vary.

3. Answers will vary.

Final Exam Answers

1.   Allies. Enemies of the Axis, led by Britain, United States, Russia.

2.   Axis. Enemies of the Allies, led by Germany, Italy, Japan.

3.   Among the Allied Powers, the USSR suffered the greatest number of casualties: 18,000,000.

4.   Among the Axis Powers, Germany suffered the greatest number of casualties: 4,200,000.

5.   World War II was mainly a battle between Germany and the USSR.

6.   The Eastern Front was fought mainly in East Europe and mainly involved Russia and Germany.

7.   More than 28 million were killed on the Eastern Front. This was 75% of all the deaths in the war.

8.   The other major fronts of World War II included the Pacific Theater, Western Front, North Africa, the Italian Campaign, Southeast Asia, and the Balkans.

9.   Fascism. The political philosophy that is no philosophy at all. Do whatever appears necessary. It is derived from the law of the Roman Empire.

10. Socialism. An economic and political system under which virtually everything and everyone is owned and controlled by government agencies.

11. Besides the Jews, the Nazis also murdered prisoners of war, the aged, the sick, homosexuals, Slavs, Serbs, Czechs, Italians, Poles, Ukrainians, and many others including, of course, anyone they thought might be plotting against them.

12. According to Uncle Eric, Stalin murdered more people than Hitler. Stalin murdered 42.7 million people compared to about 20.9 million murdered by Hitler.

13. Stalin's Order #270 said that all Soviet troops taken prisoner would be considered traitors and shot, and their wives would be sent to labor camps. In effect, Stalin made his whole army into a suicide army.

14. Hitler wanted to take over Europe, which totals 6.6 percent of the earth's land surface.

15. In keeping with the works of Lenin and Marx, Stalin wanted to conquer the world.

16. At the maximum extent of his reach, in 1942, Hitler controlled about 4 percent of the world.

17. The Soviet Socialists had conquered 16 percent of the world.

18. Britain had conquered 22 percent of the world.

19. President Franklin Roosevelt sided with China in World War II. The Chinese Kuomintang murdered 10,214,000; the Japanese regime murdered 5,964,000.

20. The Red Chinese took over China in 1949; the Red Chinese murdered 35 million.

21. In terms of the number of people murdered and the geographical proximity, Stalin was the greater threat to the United States.

22. By the expression, "The sun never sets on the British Empire" is meant that London held stolen territories around the globe so somewhere in the British Empire it was always daylight.

23. Much of the British army and navy were not available for defense of Britain because it was scattered all over the world trying to hang onto all the nations London had conquered.

24. When history books are written by the victors, then history will generally be slanted in favor of the victors. The other side of the story, those who were defeated, is seldom favorably told.

25. The British people gave the world the system of the old British Common Law and the Industrial Revolution, which resulted in civilization as we know it today.

26. The Anglo-Saxonists believed that the white British and Americans were natural allies, superior to others, and entitled to rule the world.

27. Blitzkrieg. Lightning war. A German term meaning a swift, powerful strike spearheaded by tanks and aircraft.

28. In 1917, U.S. President Wilson abandoned neutrality and joined the Allies, which caused victory for the Allies.

29. The Germans wanted revenge because the Treaty of Versailles so impoverished them that they were desperate to escape their situation.

30. The nine governments that have been behind most of the worst wars since the Middle Ages are: Beijing, Berlin, London, Moscow, Paris, Rome, Tokyo, Vienna, and Washington D.C.

31. September 1, 1939, is the date usually targeted as the start of World War II with the German invasion of Poland.

32. Uncle Eric says that the invasion of Manchuria by Japan in 1931 marks the real beginning of World War II.

33. The Spanish Civil War, which began in July 1936, was a preview of the conflict between fascism and socialism that would eventually be played out between Germany and Russia on the Eastern Front.

34. The main conflict of World War II was the Eastern Front, a conflict between Germany and Russia.

35. "Appeasement" was the idea that if the German Nazis and Italian fascists were allowed to take a small amount of territory, then they would be satisfied and would not try to take huge amounts of territory, as the governments of Britain, France, and Russia had done for centuries.

36. In 1937 Hitler formally declared an end to the Treaty of Versailles.

37. In August 1939, Berlin and Moscow agreed to the Soviet-German Nonaggression Pact in which Hitler and Stalin agreed not to attack each other. This also said that Berlin would get a large part of Poland for its new empire, and Moscow could have the rest of Poland, plus Finland, Estonia, Latvia, and Lithuania.

38. Moscow conquered more territory between 1919 and 1940 than Berlin.

39. This meant all the British and French colonies around the world would again find themselves at war with the Germans.

40. In September 1940, Rome, Berlin, and Tokyo signed the Tripartite Pact in which they agreed that if one of them went to war with someone, they all would. Alliances is the deadly idea represented by the Tripartite Pact. Rome, Berlin, and Tokyo agreed that if one got into a war, they all would come to the defense of the other, which escalated the war into a world war.

41. Fascism was the European political philosophy that was popular for thousands of years and still popular in Europe when World War II broke out.

42. World War II was mostly a battle between fascists and socialists, and with the USG's help, the socialists won.

43. The Higgins boat was invented in the U.S. to land troops and equipment on beaches. The Germans had none. As a result the Germans had to capture a port to land troops and equipment. Because they were unable to invade Britain by boat, the Germans had to resort to an air war, known as the Battle of Britain.

44. Russia is too big, too cold, too wet, and too flat to successfully invade. The only months available for fighting a full-scale war are the three summer months.

45. The last person to mount a successful winter invasion of Russia was Genghis Khan in 1236 AD, and it took him four years.

46. The Russian defensive strategy is to keep retreating until winter arrives. The enemy must then confront severe weather and fragile supply lines. When the snow melts, the Russians cut the supply lines and attack.

47. Uncle Eric says that September 12, 1941 is the most important date of World War II because the snow began falling in Russia and, as a result, Germany became unable to conquer Russia. The war was winding down.

48. Most people believe the U.S. government entered World War II on December 7, 1941.

49. Uncle Eric believes that if Hitler and Stalin fought each other, they would so weaken each other that neither would emerge a threat to the rest of the world for some time to come.

50. According to Uncle Eric, "America's entry into the war on December 7th was not needed because the German war machine was already in deep trouble on September 12th, when the first snow fell in Russia." Knowing the sequence of events demonstrates that many of the history lessons that teach about the necessity of the United States joining World War II are wrong. The war was ending without U.S. involvement.

51. Japan was the chief naval power in the Orient by the 1930s.

52. The *Panay* incident was significant because the USG was involved in this incident in China, yet Japan was sending a clear message to the USG to get out of China. According to Uncle Eric, the *Panay* incident in 1937 marked the actual entry of America into World War II. The *Panay* incident illustrates these two deadly ideas that lead to war: global protection and interests.

53. Uncle Eric says the United States was the undisputed industrial giant of the world, more powerful in economic and military terms than any other nation. Also, the Axis only controlled 3.3% of the earth's land surface while the British had conquered 22% and the Russians 16%. It didn't make economic sense that the Axis could outfight the United States or the Allies.

54. The Atlantic Charter was a loosely worded agreement for the governments of Britain and the U.S. to work together toward peace, economic advancement, freedom of travel, and "general security."

55. Roosevelt agreed to commit American forces to a war, even if Japan attacked British, not United States, territory. The agreement, which was hidden, was not approved by Congress, which is required by the U.S. Constitution. It also violated the Neutrality Act.

56. Logistics are important in a war because the side with the ability to move quickly and transport the most supplies to the battlefield would be the winner.

57. In 1941, the chief supplier of oil, iron, and other necessary resources to Japan was the United States.

58. McCollum's eight-point plan was intended to provoke Japan into committing an overt act of war against the U.S. He believed this would then change the minds of the American people about getting involved in the war.

59. FDR, by starting the Flying Tigers, had declared war on the Japanese before the Japanese had attacked Pearl Harbor.

60. On June 9, 1941, Admiral Kimmel met with Roosevelt to tell him about a possible Japanese attack on Pearl Harbor. Kimmel was concerned because he didn't have enough planes or anti-aircraft guns to protect the fleet.

61. In anticipation of a possible Japanese attack, Admiral Kimmel sent his fleet to the Prokofiev Seamount to thwart any possible attack, which Kimmel believed would happen from that location. But the USG ordered Kimmel and his fleet back to Pearl Harbor.

62. The Japanese launched their planes from the Prokofiev Seamount.

63. Executive Order No. 9066 was signed on February 19, 1942, and required U.S. Army troops to round up persons of Japanese ancestry.

64. Seventy percent of the Japanese placed in U.S. concentration camps were United States citizens.

65. The story of the Panzer Lehr Division is important because, even though the Panzer Lehr tanks were superior to the American Sherman tanks, the 45 Panzer Lehr tanks were no match against 2000 Allied planes. And the most important part of the story is that the German government was unable to produce many replacements. So, even though the technology was superior, the Germans couldn't reproduce that technology.

66. Italy changed sides in 1943, joining the Allies.

67. In the Pacific Theater the war was primarily the U.S. versus Japan.

68. The European Theater had two main fronts: The Western Front and Eastern Front

    a. The Western Front was mainly Britain, parts of France, and later the U.S., against Germany.

    b. The Eastern Front was Germany versus the USSR.

        (The European Theater also included the Italian Campaign in Italy and other minor conflicts, like the Balkans.)

69. The main battlefield of the war was the Eastern Front, between Hitler and Stalin.

70. The Battle at Stalingrad (now Volgograd) on the Eastern Front was the worst in all of human history. It lasted five months and killed 1,110,000.

71. The biggest battle on the Western Front was the D-Day landings on the Normandy beaches. Except for small pockets of resistance, that battle was over in 72 hours. Deaths of Allied troops numbered less than 2,500. German and civilian deaths are unknown but were probably not more than 10,000.

72. Hitler's attack on Stalin in June 1941 was the single largest military operation in all of human history. Of the Wehrmacht's 209 divisions, Hitler used 144 to attack the Soviet Union.

73. Hitler could not beat both Russia and Britain. Britain's navy was superior to Hitler's and the Russian artillery was greater than Hitler's. Also, Hitler was going to fight on Russian soil during a Russian winter.

74. Jeannette Rankin was the only member of Congress who voted against declaring war on the Axis. She also voted against participation in World War I and led protest marches against the Vietnam War.

75. If you look at the production side of the war, Germany was clearly outclassed. Economically, Hitler could not win.

76. Hitler opted for quality rather than quantity in World War II, as well as frequent design changes. German quality was great but they couldn't produce enough. Also, the frequent design changes meant they weren't producing enough parts to repair the myriad types of vehicles they were using.

77. Without oil, tanks don't run, planes don't fly, and ships don't sail.

78. The Allies had 90 percent of the oil and the Axis had 3 percent.

79. By 1944 Germany was so short of aluminum and other metals that the new Heinkel 162 jet fighter had to be made mostly of wood.

80. The Brookings Institution reported that Germany, Italy, and their allies were short of lead, copper, cobalt, and most other industrial raw materials needed to make and operate weapons, as well as being short of food.

81. The Germans had to move their logistics troops first, to get the transportation route in place so they could then move their tanks, planes, and infantry. Usually it is the other way around.

82. Most people believe the invasion of Normandy was to liberate France and the rest of Western Europe from the Germans. The real purpose for the invasion of Normandy was to open a second front to help Stalin who wanted German troops drawn away from the Eastern Front.

83. The Moscow Declaration said that the Germans would be forced to pay reparations for the war again, which was just what the German people feared might happen.

84. The Battle of Stalingrad took place in September 1942 and was the worst battle in all of human history, killing 1.1 million people in five months. At the conclusion of the battle, Germany was losing the war.

85. Franklin Roosevelt called for Unconditional Surrender on January 24, 1943, one week before the Battle of Stalingrad ended. As a result, the war continued for two more years with men, women, and children dying at the rate of a million a month.

86. The other historic case of Unconditional Surrender found by Lord Maurice Hankey was the war between the Romans and the Carthaginians. The Romans entirely destroyed Carthage.

87. The Japanese were given the same terms for surrender as the Germans – Unconditional Surrender.

88. In DAY ONE, Peter Wyden states that the atomic bomb was dropped on Japan as a demonstration to frighten the Russians.

89. Truman halted Lend Lease aid to the USSR on May 12, 1945. The date is significant because it marked the beginning of the Cold War.

90. The Russian people were given modern weapons to fight the Germans in World War I. Instead, they used the weapons on the Czar who was overthrown and killed. It was the 1917 Russian Revolution.

91. The socialists came into power following the 1917 Russian Revolution.

92. Operation Keelhaul was the program by which the Allies returned two million captured Soviet rebels in German uniforms to the Soviet government toward the end of the war to be executed or imprisoned.

93. Soviet troops invaded Afghanistan in 1979.

94. The Soviet Empire began to collapse in November 1989 with the tearing down of the Berlin Wall, about nine months after the Soviets fled Afghanistan.

95. Joseph Stalin emerged as the most powerful person in the Old World following World War II.

96. Stalin directly controlled a sixth of all the land on earth.

97. The 1947 Truman Doctrine allowed the U.S. government to give money, weapons, and military training to anyone who claimed to be anti-Soviet. It stayed in effect until the collapse of the Soviet Empire in the 1990s.

98. By the year 2000, the U.S. sphere of influence comprised more than 100 countries, the largest empire the world has ever known.

99. The root cause of terrorist attacks against the U.S. is revenge against the U.S. from the victims of U.S. backed countries.

100. The two laws that make peace, liberty, and prosperity possible are: 1) Do all you have agreed to do (this is the basis of contract law), and 2) do not encroach on other persons or their property (this is the basis of tort law and some criminal law).

Published by Bluestocking Press

Uncle Eric Books by Richard J. Maybury

UNCLE ERIC TALKS ABOUT PERSONAL, CAREER, AND FINANCIAL SECURITY
WHATEVER HAPPENED TO PENNY CANDY?
WHATEVER HAPPENED TO JUSTICE?
ARE YOU LIBERAL? CONSERVATIVE? OR CONFUSED?
ANCIENT ROME: HOW IT AFFECTS YOU TODAY
EVALUATING BOOKS: WHAT WOULD THOMAS JEFFERSON THINK ABOUT THIS?
THE MONEY MYSTERY
THE CLIPPER SHIP STRATEGY
THE THOUSAND YEAR WAR IN THE MIDEAST
WORLD WAR I: THE REST OF THE STORY
WORLD WAR II: THE REST OF THE STORY

Bluestocking Guides (study guides for the Uncle Eric books)
by Jane A. Williams and/or Kathryn Daniels

A BLUESTOCKING GUIDE: BUILDING A PERSONAL MODEL FOR SUCCESS (based on UNCLE ERIC TALKS ABOUT...)
A BLUESTOCKING GUIDE: ECONOMICS (based on WHATEVER HAPPENED TO PENNY CANDY?)
A BLUESTOCKING GUIDE: JUSTICE (based on WHATEVER HAPPENED TO JUSTICE?)
A BLUESTOCKING GUIDE: POLITICAL PHILOSOPHIES (based on ARE YOU LIBERAL? CONSERVATIVE? OR CONFUSED?)
A BLUESTOCKING GUIDE: ANCIENT ROME (based on ANCIENT ROME: HOW IT AFFECTS YOU TODAY)
A BLUESTOCKING GUIDE: SOLVING THE MONEY MYSTERY (based on THE MONEY MYSTERY)
A BLUESTOCKING GUIDE: APPLYING THE CLIPPER SHIP STRATEGY (based on THE CLIPPER SHIP STRATEGY)
A BLUESTOCKING GUIDE: THE MIDEAST WAR (based on THE THOUSAND YEAR WAR IN THE MIDEAST)
A BLUESTOCKING GUIDE: WORLD WAR I: THE REST OF THE STORY
A BLUESTOCKING GUIDE: WORLD WAR II: THE REST OF THE STORY

Each Study Guide includes some or all of the following:
    1) chapter-by-chapter comprehension questions and answers
    2) application questions and answers
    3) research activities
    4) essay assignments
    5) thought questions
    6) final exam

More Bluestocking Press Titles

LAURA INGALLS WILDER AND ROSE WILDER LANE HISTORICAL TIMETABLE
ECONOMICS: A FREE MARKET READER edited by Jane Williams & Kathryn Daniels
CAPITALISM FOR KIDS: GROWING UP TO BE YOUR OWN BOSS by Karl Hess
BUSINESS FOR KIDS: EXPLAINING COMMON SENSE REALITIES BEHIND BASIC BUSINESS PRINCIPLES
    by Kathryn Daniels & Anthony Joseph

The Bluestocking Press Catalog
Includes varied and interesting selections of historical toys and crafts, historical documents, economics, and more.

Order any of the above items from Bluestocking Press by phone or online.

Bluestocking Press
web site: www.BluestockingPress.com
Phone: 800-959-8586
email: CustomerService@BluestockingPress.com